"Like a wilderness guide, Jill Crainshaw leads us through poetry and politics, science and spirituality, to open our eyes to the wonder of God's active presence all around us. Drawing from a deep well of sacramental theology, Crainshaw shows us the profound relationship between our sacred rituals and our daily lives, that we may live more mindfully, passionately, and faithfully. Her book is a great gift to preachers, liturgists, and all people who seek to love God—and God's world—with all their heart, soul, mind, and strength."

—Kimberly Bracken Long, Editor, *Call to Worship: Liturgy, Music, Preaching and the Arts*

"Reading *When I in Awesome Wonder* is a sheer delight! Rich in stories, metaphors, and imagery, this book takes the holy stuff of worship (bread, wine, water, hope, awe, relationships) and grounds it in the everyday stuff of life (food sources and food scarcity, water sources and water contamination, hopelessness around the great issues of our day, etc.). The conversation between these two greatly enhances how we view what we do in worship and reorients us to what we might do differently in worship, but it also allows us to see how the 'stuff' of our everyday lives is truly holy—given to us for the work of God in our communities and in the world. As Crainshaw notes, worship then 'orients us toward God, the world and others in life-savoring and life-saving ways.'"

—Kathy Black
    Gerald Kennedy Chair of Homiletics and Liturgics
    Claremont School of Theology

"Jill Crainshaw has offered us all a rich gift. Like a wise teacher, she has invited us to reexamine the ordinary experiences of our lives and find the extraordinary love of God within them. Like a compassionate prophet, she has drawn attention to the injustices of our world near and far and invited us to respond in small and large ways. Like an insightful poet, she offers texts that invite our repeated reading and our concerted contemplation. Like a loving pastor, she has interpreted scriptures and rites for us in provocative and practical ways that draw us nearer to our earth, our neighbors, our worship, and our God. Reading *When I in Awesome Wonder* may evoke such a deep sense of 'wow,' you may not even make it to 'thank you.'"

— Todd E. Johnson
    Theological Director of the Brehm Center for Worship, Theology,
        and the Arts
    Fuller Theological Seminary

"Jill Crainshaw offers an evocative reflection on the sacramentality of everyday life and its implications for Christian worship. Each chapter retells a particular story, revealing the wonder and awe of human experience as a lens for reimagining worship. The book is provocative, instructive, and enormously inspiring, mirroring qualities that make Jill Crainshaw an exemplary liturgist, preacher, and teacher. A must-have for pastors and liturgists."

— Veronice Miles
    Visiting Professor of Preaching
    Wesley Theological Seminary

When I in Awesome Wonder
Liturgy Distilled from Daily Life

Jill Y. Crainshaw

LITURGICAL PRESS
Collegeville, Minnesota

www.litpress.org

1   2   3   4   5   6   7   8   9

Library of Congress Cataloging-in-Publication Data

Names: Crainshaw, Jill Y., 1962– author.
Title: When I in awesome wonder : liturgy distilled from daily life / Jill Y.
    Crainshaw.
Description: Collegeville, Minnesota : Liturgical Press, [2017]. | Includes
    bibliographical references.
Identifiers: LCCN 2017006250 (print) | LCCN 2017033830 (ebook) | ISBN
    9780814645826 (ebook) | ISBN 9780814645574
Subjects: LCSH: Liturgics. | Public Worship. | Spirituality—Christianity. |
    Catholic Church—Doctrines.
Classification: LCC BV178 (ebook) | LCC BV178 .C735 2017 (print) |
    DCC 264—dc23
LC record available at https://lccn.loc.gov/2017006250

In memory of

Sarah Louise Rodgers Crainshaw

(1934–2017).

She trusted in a Creator who was able to keep her from falling.

Contents

Earth Gifts

Bread.

Sourdough.

Pumpernickel.

Rye.

Old standbys—wheat and white.

Bread.

The stuff of life.

We break it, eat it, think almost nothing of it.

Golden-crusted loaves seasoned by the smell of the earth

Passed from me to you to the stranger.

We cannot live without it—

The bread or the sharing.

Grace.

Wine.

Poetry bottled and decanted.

Kiss of sweet grace on thirsty lips.

Wine.

Remembrance seasoned by the taste of the earth.

Spilled out between us,

For us,

You and me and the stranger.

We cannot live without it—

The sip of mystery or the sharing.

Grace.

Water.

Trickling.

Surging.

Moaning.

Water.

We bathe in it, fear it, plunge its murky depths.

Washing over weary feet,

Soaking chafed hands.

We cannot live without it—

The brooding Spirit,

Sea-lapped promises on sun-singed shores.

Grace.

Bread. Wine. Water.

The earth.

Broken.

Poured out.

Stirred up

In us.

Remembering that does not forget

Hungry, wilderness people

In neighborhoods, towns, cities.

Bread. Wine. Water.

Our hands

Baking, pouring, washing.

Gifts of God for the people of God.

Grace.

—Jill Crainshaw

Prelude

So we beat on, boats against the current, borne back ceaselessly into the past.

—F. Scott Fitzgerald, *The Great Gatsby*

Life is liturgy. Not just Sunday mornings or weekday prayer services. All of life. Even the commonplace happenings, places, and things of everyday living are liturgy, perhaps especially the commonplace things. Life is liturgy.

Artists, storytellers, and poets remember through words and images what they see, hear, taste, and feel in the world around them. In a similar way, I remember in these pages times in my life and ministry when poet Elizabeth Barrett Browning's words have come alive for me and I have seen the earth "crammed with heaven" and "every bush afire with God." [1] I remember in these pages times when I have experienced life as liturgy.

The biblical scholar, Walter Brueggemann, writes about the formation of Scripture as an act of imaginative remembering:

> The tradition that became Scripture is a relentless *act of imagination.* That is, the literature is not merely descriptive

---

[1] Elizabeth Barrett Browning, "Aurora Leigh," in *The Oxford Book of English Mystical Verse,* ed. D. H. S. Nicholson and A. H. E. Lee (Oxford: The Clarendon Press, 1917), also available at www.bartleby.com/236/ (accessed October 16, 2016).

of a commonsense world; it dares by artistic sensibility and risk-taking rhetoric, to posit, characterize, and vouch for a world beyond "common sense."[2]

This is the kind of remembering I undertake in this book. I explore how liturgy dares to "vouch for" in the "common sense" of everyday living the inexplicable, "beyond 'common sense'" wonders of God's presence.

The book's subtitle arises out of these acts of imaginative remembering: "liturgy distilled from everyday life." To "distill" is to "extract the essence" from something. Another definition says that to distill is "to let fall, exude, or precipitate in drops or in a wet mist."[3] I prefer the second. Sometimes our recollections of life-happenings precipitate from our memories like mist. The mist becomes a prism that refracts new and unexpected colors, textures, and meanings from what is common or familiar.

"Liturgy" is distilled from everyday life when we peer through the mist and see the sacramental and spiritual dimensions of daily actions, objects, conversations, and events. Sometimes we are aware in the moment that events happen of the liturgical or spiritual qualities of those events. Often, though, our awareness is not sparked until we look back on events. This is not unlike what happens when in weekly worship we look back on the events of Jesus' and the early church's life. We peer through the mists of years of biblical storytelling and wisdom and here and there, now and then, encounter God anew for our times as we hear ancient words and share a simple meal around a sacred "in remembrance" table.

When we remember events that we have observed or that have happened to us, we often shape and retell them as stories. How often,

---

[2] Walter Brueggemann, *An Introduction to the Old Testament: The Canon and Christian Imagination* (Louisville: Westminster John Knox Press, 2003), 9.

[3] Merriam-Webster.com (2017), s.v. "distill"; accessed June 6, 2017.

for example, have we shared with friends around a meal table stories about our growing up years or about what happened during the past week? Perhaps that is what Jesus' followers did in the weeks and months following his death and resurrection. They put the events they recalled from Jesus' life in story forms, story forms that have come to us as sacred writ, as Gospel narratives.

An intriguing thing about recalling events is that when we remember and tell stories about things we have experienced, we remember and retell more than just the facts. We "re-feel" and "re-embody" what happened, and because of that those happenings take on new life, life that surfaces as imaginative storying.[4] We create and re-create meaning by weaving together a story that makes sense to us for the time when we are remembering it.

That is how in this book I have distilled liturgy from everyday life. The narratives I share here are from events I have observed or experienced. They are acts of imaginative remembering because my recollection of them has stirred for me new understandings of the liturgical dimensions present in the events. I story these events anew in these chapters, reflecting in my telling of them the unexpected meanings they have come to hold for me as I have recalled them again and yet again over time.

Does this mean that the stories I tell here are not true? No, but imaginative remembering, like living a life, is an imperfect exercise. I celebrate with gratitude the people and places I remembered and storied again as I wrote this book. But I realize that my recollections are personal and contextual and to some extent ambiguous. What I remember here is shaped by how I use words and in some instances by my inability to find adequate words to capture the power or beauty of an event or place. I seek grace in advance where my storying stutters

---

[4] E. Keightley and M. Pickering, *The Mnemonic Imagination: Remembering as Creative Practice* (New York: Palgrave Macmillan, 2012), 14–42.

or stumbles. That, too, is part of the distillation process. Memories mature over time. Some details fade into the background while others take on unexpected prominence. The liturgy that is life shifts and changes and sometimes becomes clearer to us as we continue to remember, retell, and remember again.

The haunting last lines of F. Scott Fitzgerald's *The Great Gatsby* capture the multidimensional power of imaginative remembering: "Gatsby believed in the green light, the orgiastic future that year by year recedes before us. It eluded us then, but that's no matter— tomorrow we will run faster, stretch out our arms farther. . . . And then one fine morning—So we beat on, boats against the current, borne back ceaselessly into the past."[5] With these closing lines, Fitzgerald reminds us of how past, present, and future are intertwined in human life.

Past, present, and future are also intertwined in our remembering in our liturgies. Contemporary author Annie Liontas says about this ending of *The Great Gatsby:* "As spare and stripped down as the narrative purports to be, there is an elliptical nature to Fitzgerald's third novel. It refuses to say what it's saying, or it says it over and over, and still you can't quite hold on to it. Much like prayer."[6] Life has this elliptical nature. Liturgy too. Both refuse to say what they are saying while at the same time saying it over and over. This means that to search out through imaginative remembering—through storying— what life is saying is to engage in a prayerful act. It is to engage in a prayerful act whereby we distill liturgy from daily life.

I have been blessed by a calling that has carried me out upon many vocational seas. The people I have encountered as pastor, chaplain,

---

[5] F. Scott Fitzgerald, *The Great Gatsby* (New York: Scribner, 2004), 180.

[6] Annie Liontas, "The Month of Fitzgerald: So We Beat On: The Last Line of *The Great Gatsby,*" *Scribner Magazine,* http://www.scribnermagazine.com/2015/04/so-we-beat-on-on-the great-gatsbys-last-lines/ (accessed June 6, 2017).

and professor—the people with whom I have shared a lifeboat—have enlivened my perceptions of life and my understandings of faith. Some of these people appear in these pages. At least, my recollections about them do. Again, I repent in advance for evidences of my faulty remembering even as I offer gratitude for the holy ground on which I have been blessed to stand with so many to taste and see God's mysteries.

To be attentive to liturgies wherever we are is to be attentive to God's mysteries. It is to be attentive to how God is present wherever we are. My hope is that readers will join me in listening and looking for the liturgical dimensions of their own life stories. The remembering and writing process has made me more aware *in the moment,* as life happenings unfold, of where liturgy—God's work with God's people—lives in my life story. I hope something similar can happen for those who read this book.

Chapter 1

Awed by Your Signs

Praise is due to you, O God, in Zion; and to you shall vows be performed,

> O you who answer prayer! . . .

By your strength you established the mountains; you are girded with might.

You silence the roaring of the seas, the roaring of their waves, the tumult of the peoples.

Those who live at earth's farthest bounds are awed by your signs; you make the gateways of the morning and the evening shout for joy.

You visit the earth and water it, you greatly enrich it; the river of God is full of water; you provide the people with grain, for so you have prepared it.

You water its furrows abundantly, settling its ridges, softening it with showers, and blessing its growth.

You crown the year with your bounty; your wagon tracks overflow with richness.

The pastures of the wilderness overflow, the hills gird themselves with joy, the meadows clothe themselves with flocks, the valleys deck themselves with grain, they shout and sing together for joy.

—Psalm 65:1-2; 6-13 (NRSV)

I baptized Martha in the river. We had to ride in four-wheel-drive vehicles to get to the place she had chosen. The day was clear and hot, one of those summer afternoons when crickets, katydids, and cicadas were tuned up and setting the air abuzz with their serenade.

I was distracted. The snake that had slithered by a few weeks earlier when we baptized Susan in a different part of the river? It had haunted my dreams the night before. Deacon John had seen that snake too. He and I had agreed to keep the serpent sighting a secret since no one else seemed to have noticed, but on the day of Martha's baptism, I was on high alert for a tell-tale flash of black and silver in the water.

I loved river baptisms, but, wary of snakes on this day, I could understand why the advent of indoor plumbing had prompted so many immersion baptism congregations to construct indoor baptisteries. Our 175-year-old church had never had any baptistery other than the family of rivers in our generous watershed.

Martha was not distracted. Her silver-white hair reached out for the wind, and "sunlight poured from her face."[1] She was elated. For her, this baptism was a dream sixty years in the making. "I want to be baptized like Jesus was in the Jordan," Martha said to me one Sunday morning. Martha's "Jordan" was a spot on the East River where, she said, "my grandma and maybe even my great-grandma fished for trout."

The family fishing hole is where we gathered that Sunday afternoon, Martha and I and about twenty-five church members. After disembarking from trucks and Jeeps, we followed the river along an overgrown trail until we came upon a place where the path spilled into an opening in the brush. There the river awaited us, expansive and sparkling, just beyond a sandy beach.

Martha, Deacon John, and I waded into the water. Martha was wearing jeans and a t-shirt and a pair of white tennis shoes purchased for

---

[1] See Matthew 17:1-3, *The Message: The Bible in Contemporary Language*, Eugene H. Peterson, trans. (NavPress, 2014).

the occasion. A church member on the beach began to strum her guitar, and the community sang an old hymn, "Shall We Gather at the River," as the three of us made our way into a deep pool just beyond the shore.

When the singing ended, another church member read from Psalm 65, a favorite of Martha's. The ancient words danced all around us as the cicada-cricket-katydid summer trio jazzed in the background: "The river of God is full of water . . . [the meadows and valleys] shout and sing together for joy."

A three-day deluge just a few days before had ended the spring drought. On Martha's baptism day, the South River was full of water and full of God's presence.

Then, just as I lifted a hand to offer a blessing over Martha and lower her into the water, I heard the sounds of Sunday afternoon merriment in the distance. I looked upriver. Two canoes appeared from around the bend, the people in them fishing and laughing as the current carried them along the watery path. They grew quiet when they saw the three of us in the water.

Unplanned but Spirit-prompted, our church group on the shore began to sing again, though quieter this time to accompany my prayer over the water. Then, I spoke ancient baptismal words—"I baptize you, Martha, child of God, in the name of God who creates, God who redeems, and God who sustains"—and Martha dipped down beneath the river's surface. When she splashed up out of the water, dripping and laughing, the canoers waved and joined our church members and the river itself in shouting out and singing for joy.

It was a moment of wonder and awe.

That baptismal moment has stayed with me more than two decades now and seasons one of my core theological and spiritual questions: What stirs wonder in our world today? Another question accompanies this one: How can we revitalize the link between wonder and worship?

That we should be awed by a summer insect symphony or a river's rain-sated cry while seeing and hearing a beloved child of God plunge into the watery promises of grace did not surprise me. But awe has many faces and what did surprise me was the unexpected presence of more than one of those faces as Martha's life story met God's mysteries in the family fishing hole that day. Martha's East River baptism "like Jesus" reminded me. When awe and wonder meet in worship, worshipers have the opportunity to encounter new dimensions and depths of God's love and grace in human lives.

Martha was her farming family's oldest child and primary caregiver. By the time she waded into the river on that day of her baptism, she had leaned in close and heard with her ears and heart the groans of a brother wounded in a hunting accident. She had spent nights by the bedside of her mother as she faded away into death. She had seen baby lambs on the family farm burst through womb-waters of mamas who died soon after. And echoing Psalm 65, she had seen her family's "wagon tracks overflow with richness" as nieces and nephews were born and as God "provided [all of them] with grain."

Martha's life reflects what is true about human life and about the awe we experience when we draw near to listen to and look at our own lives or the lives of others. Awe is bitter and sweet because life is bitter and sweet. This is the theological wisdom Martha taught me. She never used the word "awe" to talk about God or faith or her life, but her attitude of reverence for the earth, her generous care for people, and her faithful presence leading worship in the choir at church—even the peace that dwelled in her eyes and the unruly swirl of her silver-gray hair—embodied awe. Martha had been intimate with the depth and breadth, the expansive joy, and the profound sorrow of what life has to offer, and she knew. Life is bitter and sweet. But Martha's experiences of life's bitterness had not embittered her. Instead, the sweep of her life experiences seemed to deepen her reverence for the gifts of each day.

Martha lived in awe of life even though she carried in her body and soul bittersweet complexities of life. Yes, Martha's heart and body

had been bared both to beauty and to pain, so she knew. Life is both
to be feared and reverenced because fear and reverence live together
in human stories as brother and sister, intimate and inseparable even
if often discordant.

And Martha yearned to be baptized. I was not certain of all of
what she meant by her insistence on being baptized in the river "like
Jesus was." Perhaps she wanted to experience a part of her life as she
imagined Jesus had experienced his. Or maybe she wanted to sub-
merge the full range of the life experiences she carried in her bones
in baptism's promises of grace and hope. Perhaps she wanted to join
her life, if but for a moment, to a river's inscrutable wisdom about
life and death. Perhaps Martha wanted to be immersed in whatever
micro- and macro- organismic possibilities dwell beneath a river's
surface or that flow out from a river to the sea. Or it could be that
she longed to be wonderstruck by the depths of a river in all of its
physical and symbolic dimensions.

I suspect Martha's request had to do with all of those "perhapses"
and more, but what I heard as most urgent in Martha's baptismal
request was her yearning to mark in an earthy, physical way her belief that all of her life had been saturated by God's presence. Martha
intuited that being baptized like Jesus, in a river teeming with slither-
ing snakes and childhood memories, serenaded by whippoorwills
and tree frogs—being baptized in the river in some mysterious way
both immersed the complex whole of her bittersweet life in God's
grace and announced her belief that she had never not been immersed
in God's grace. She understood herself to be, like Jesus was, God's
beloved child.

And in that was the richness of the theological wisdom Martha
shared with me by asking me to baptize her in that river. Martha was
acquainted with death. She knew about drought years on the farm
when the rains did not fall and seeds could not take root, and she knew
from her time at her mother's bedside how cancer can ravage a human

body. Martha's baptism invited me as a young pastor to think more deeply than I ever had both about those life places where rain softens and blesses the earth and those life places where waters run dry.

Can wonder's voice be heard in hospital emergency rooms where the only obvious sounds are beeping heart machines and whispered words of deaths foretold? What does wonder sound or look like in windowless buildings where assembly line workers give long hours in exchange for minimum-wage pay? Can we experience wonder while doing laundry or cajoling children to brush their teeth or paying monthly electricity bills? Does wonder stand with us when we protest on the steps of our state's capitol building? Does wonder live on dangerous streets where mamas stand guard against sinister strangers? What is wonder-inspiring about those rivers that flow unseen beneath city streets only to be noticed if the kitchen faucet spits out dirty water? Can we tap into wonder in the countless places across the globe where water is scarce?

These questions are micro-versions of what many theologians, anthropologists, ecologists, and others are asking on macro levels. The popular religious author, Diana Butler Bass, describes the contemporary situation this way:

> We now live in a theologically flattened world. We have discovered that we are fully capable of creating the terrors of hell right here and no longer need a lake of fire to prove the existence of evil . . . and that no deity appears to be sending miracles to fix the mess we are in. [2]

But Bass does not stop with this. "If hell has moved next door," she says, "perhaps heaven has too." [3]

---

[2] Diana Butler Bass, *Grounded: Finding God in the World: A Spiritual Revolution* (New York: HarperOne, 2015), ebook.

[3] Ibid.

As I read Bass's words, Martha's baptism comes to mind. So, too, do wonder and awe. Perhaps God is somehow with us in life's hellish and heavenly realities, and by wrestling with that truth we can discover anew our human capacity to experience and cultivate awe and wonder and even for worship.

Wonder and awe are apt descriptors for worship and for everyday spirituality. Both worship and everyday life are made up of a strange intermingling of delight and terror, bitter and sweet, astonishment and attention in the face of the sacred or sublime. Worship and the human capacity to birth wonder and awe in all of their fullness is the subject of this book.[4]

Wonder and awe are what Martha, those canoers, our church community and I experienced on the river that summer day. The fleeting convergence of the scenic serpent-inhabited river, human yearning for divine encounter, biblical stories with images of other sacred rivers, and communal eruption of laughter and singing got our *a*ttention— both physical and spiritual. We were wonderstruck, and in ways that we did not even give voice to at the time, that wonderstruck moment shaped our life *in*tention, our ideas about how we are to respond to the bittersweet realities we encounter in our lives.

Philosopher Jerome A. Miller's perspective on wonder energizes my own. Wonder, Miller says, seizes our imaginations and stirs within us a desire to encounter the unknown—what is other or strange to us—as it is embedded in the multiplicity of worlds in which we live and work and worship and play.[5] In other words, wonder opens our

---

[4] As Rembert G. Weakland notes on the book jacket for Don Saliers's *Worship Come to Its Senses* (Nashville: Abingdon, 1996), Saliers considers awe as one of four "senses" of God along with delight, truth, and hope. Saliers considers why "wonderment, surprise, truthfulness, and expectancy" are so often "missing or diminished in Christian liturgy today."

[5] Jerome A. Miller, *In the Throe of Wonder: Intimations of the Sacred in a Post-Modern World* (New York: SUNY Press, 1992), 33.

eyes, ears, and hearts to those unexpected or overlooked or unfamiliar facts of our everyday lives.

Another philosopher, Mary-Jane Rubenstein says this about wonder: "wonder . . . responds to a destabilizing and unassimilable interruption in the ordinary course of things, an uncanny opening, rift or wound in the everyday."[6]

Together, Miller's and Rubenstein's understandings stir an idea central to this book: To wonder at and in our world is a sacred act because wonder interrupts our ordinary responses to life. Wonder makes us curious anew about familiar events and places and things so that we see in them elements or qualities that are unexpected. Wonder creates an uncanny opening or rift that lets us see in everyday things the mysteries of God. In fact, this description of wonder may be a fitting description for what we call in worship "sacramental." Many scholars and worship leaders speak about sacraments as outward and visible signs of invisible and inward grace. What if this means that sacraments—made up of the earth's everyday elements such as water and bread and wine—are, like wonder, interruptions or uncanny openings or rifts or even wounds in the everyday that reveal the depths of the everyday itself because they reveal God within the everyday?

Take the sacramental use of bread in worship as an example: What God-encounters are sparked when we bless and break a loaf of bread in worship and then say as we share it with each other, "the body of Christ, given for you"? Bread as symbol or sacrament in worship is indeed a powerful link to the theological wonder of how God is present through Christ. But the bread is more than a symbolic placeholder for the real meaning of Jesus' life, death, and resurrection. Bread is bread, and bread's flour-yeast-water simplicity and mystery is in its very earthiness an awe-inspiring link to God's presence. Bread

---

[6] Mary-Jane Rubenstein, *Strange Wonder: The Closure of Metaphysics and the Opening of Awe* (New York: Columbia University Press, 2008), 10.

comes from the earth and becomes bread in part because of God's creative presence in sun and soil, the sweat of human brows, and the bread-baking wisdom of human hands. The "bread of life"—used to refer to Jesus in John's Gospel—and the "bread of life"—used by some to refer to a basic and essential food staple—are intimately connected. And when we break bread in worship, we interrupt both divine and everyday understandings. We create an uncanny rift in what we think we know about God and life. We wound the bread and reveal the life-giving truths of the bread.

What this means in terms of the sacramentality of Christian worship is that the bread, wine, water, and oil central to Sunday worship do more than symbolize or point to religious truths or meanings that exist deeper than or outside of their physical reality. The physical "stuff" of our worship is in itself a source of wonder: the bread, wine, water, and oil are harbingers of God-with-us because they open us up both to life-essential and awe-inspiring worlds of meaning. God somehow inhabits creation—life's matter—and that matter in its own peculiar way announces God's presence and makes God's presence accessible.[7] To wonder—to marvel—at the stuff of life is to worship.[8] And to wonder at the stuff of worship Sunday after Sunday is to embrace life.

To put it in Miller's terms, wonder is a hinge or threshold between encountering God at church on Sunday and encountering God at work or at the grocery store on Monday.[9] Wonder stretches out and

---

[7] Ibid., 48.

[8] Søren Kierkegaard, *Three Discourses on Imagined Occasions:* "the expression of wonder is worship. And wonder is an ambiguous state of mind which comprises fear and bliss. Worship therefore is mingled fear and bliss all at once." Quoted in Celia Deane-Drummond, *Wonder and Wisdom: Conversations in Science, Spirituality, and Theology* (Philadelphia: Templeton Foundation Press, 2006), 6. See also Søren Kierkegaard, *Three Discourses on Imagined Occasions*, ed. and trans. Howard V. Hong and Edna H. Hong (Princeton, NJ: Princeton University Press, 1993), 18.

[9] Miller, *Throe of Wonder*, 33.

across the gap to many faith communities' experience between the matter—the stuff—of Sunday worship and the matter—the stuff—of everyday life and invites us to venture beyond our limited and often overly nostalgic shallows of faith into unknown watery depths.

Wonder stands at the doorway, at the threshold, between everyday living and cosmic mystery and asks: Why are we here? What dwells beyond what we usually see and hear in life's rivers and fields and forests, on life's city streets and in life's suburban neighborhoods? But wonder does not only point us away from or beyond rivers and neighborhoods—*beyond* the stuff—of the here and now; wonder also marvels at all that is right here in the places where we live and work, the stuff of life that presents itself to be known, touched, tasted, experienced both in familiar and unfamiliar ways by us. Wonder beckons us to explore—to savor—every millimeter and millisecond of our lives and surroundings, expecting to experience in and through them God's intimate and expansive presence.[10]

My hope for this book is that readers and, perhaps by way of them, communities of faith will be captured again by earthy, everyday wonder and experiment with what it means to move back and forth across that threshold between what we too often see as separate and incompatible domains—between heaven and earth, the church and the world, the here and not yet, what is known and what is as yet mystery.

I learned as a young pastor, serving a congregation in the mountains of Virginia, the power of place, places, and people for culti-

---

[10] See Miller's chapter on "Wonder as Hinge," *In the Throe of Wonder*, 33–52. See also Mary-Jane Rubenstein, *Strange Wonder: The Closure of Metaphysics and the Opening of Awe (Insurrections: Critical Studies in Religion, Politics, and Culture)* (New York: Columbia University Press, 2010); Jane Bennett, *Vibrant Matter: A Political Ecology of Things* (Durham, NC: Duke University Press, 2010); Catherine Keller, *The Face of the Deep: A Theology of Becoming* (New York: Routledge, 2003). For more on liminality, see the work of the ritual theorists Victor Turner and Arthur Van Gennep.

vating wonder and cultivating life-giving and life-transforming experiences of God's presence. The good factory-working and farming people of that community offered generous patience as I learned to preach and pray and to preside at Communion and committee meetings. They also taught me to milk cows, shovel sheep manure onto church-ground shrubs, pick and can green beans, and wait in silence at the base of pine trees for a committee of vultures to fly in at sunset to roost (and yes, a group of vultures resting in trees is called a committee, a fact that can altogether transform a pastor's perspective on church committees). Together, my church community and I faced the sometimes delightful, sometimes terrifying, wonder of it all—in-church liturgies, down-by-the riverside liturgies, garden-bean-row liturgies, and hospital bedside liturgies.[11]

This book celebrates the vitality of liturgies distilled from everyday life. In other words, the book explores how dimensions of everyday life are alive with God's grace and presence. Several questions appear along the way as provisional touchstones: How is the bread we eat everyday the same as eucharistic bread? What are the sacramental dimensions of tap water and how is tap water like baptismal water? We live, work, and play in places where people face challenges related to food and water access, economic stability, and sustainability. How does a greater awareness of the sacramental dimensions of our places contribute to our capacity to cultivate individual, communal, and even global well-being?

---

[11] See Louis Marie-Chauvet, *Symbol and Sacrament: Sacramental Reinterpretation of Christian Existence* (Collegeville, MN: Pueblo Books, 1994); Karl Rahner, *Foundations of Christian Faith: An Introduction to the Idea of Christianity*, trans. William V. Dych (New York: Crossroad, 1987); Rhodora E. Beaton, *Embodied Words; Spoken Signs: Sacramentality and the Word in Rahner and Chauvet* (Minneapolis: Augsburg Fortress Press, 2014); Jeffrey Bloechl, *Liturgy of the Neighbor: Emmanual Levinas and the Religion of Responsibility* (Pittsburgh: Duquesne, 2000).

Stories from human experiences and, in particular, places frame each chapter. For example, the chapter on food includes conversations with a bread baker, while the chapter on water includes insights from county water and wastewater treatment plant managers. The storied dimension of each chapter is vital because a primary emphasis of the book is on the place-rooted nature both of wonder and worship. What prevents wonder from becoming a kind of groundless reflective act of floating above both the horrors and delights of reality is recognizing that it emerges from actual terrain. In other words, this book is about the wonder and awe that arise from and return to human lives and stories.

Something similar can be said about worship. Worship happens in concrete places where people live and die, work and play. Bread and wine, water and oil arise from and return to the earth and its sometimes sandy, sometimes peaty soil; God's sacramental gifts arise from and return to everyday human experiences that unfold in particular and peculiar everyday places.

To reflect on worship and wonder while listening to particular stories helps us to resist temptations to settle into theological abodes that reinforce generic complacency or dominance and thus be relieved "of any sense of obligation to the messy, sociopolitical state of things."[12] This book invites readers to pay attention anew to sacramental dimensions present in the concrete realities of everyday life—in everyday activities such as working, cooking, and eating as well as drinking, playing, giving birth, rearing children, and caring for the sick and dying. The book then explores connections between these life realities and communal worship, inviting worshiping communities to imagine

---

[12] Rubenstein (*Strange Wonder* 21) references Hannah Arendt, "Ideology and Terror: A Novel Form of Government," in *The Origins of Totalitarianism* (New York: Schocken, 2004), 593–616.

and embody sacramental actions that birth justice and hope into everyday human lives, stories, and places.

This exploratory adventure begins with ancient and contemporary practices of daily prayer and considers how daily prayer rhythms, while linked to Lord's Day worship, arise from and shape everyday life. The chapters that follow consider daily life realities—food, water, birth, death, work, and play—and how they are vibrant with God's grace and presence even as they are burdened by life's injustices. The book concludes by imagining what "grounded liturgies" look and sound like and how such liturgies cultivate Gospel justice, hope, and grace. A liturgical or lyrical interlude accompanies each chapter.

Not long after Martha was baptized, she and some of the community members who were gathered by the river for the baptism started a food pantry in our church. Some in the community were resistant, but Martha and the others were insistent. Within six months, our congregation of 100 members was funding and staffing a food pantry that served over 200 people twice a month.

I journeyed on from that congregation a number of years ago, and the food pantry has since moved to another locale in the county. But sometimes even now when I buy a loaf of bread at my local grocery store or when I break bread at the Lord's table for Holy Communion, I remember those faithful food pantry workers and marvel at how the passion of a small group of folks who gathered down by the riverside was stoked (in part at least) by the Spirit of those local Jordan baptizing waters to do what they could to make God's presence real in that place.

In that place for that time, the psalmist's words echoed anew. God's wagon tracks did indeed overflow with richness. I continue with this book to wonder at how God works in our world, and I hope in the pages that follow to celebrate life-giving links between wonder and worship.

Interlude

Out of the Ordinary[1]

She did not expect it. Not in the Food Lion parking lot at sundown. Not while waiting in their 1999 Buick LeSabre for her husband to pick up a half-gallon of fat-free milk. Nothing out of the ordinary ever happened to her. Predictability was her life's plotline.

But there in the grocery store parking lot, the unexpected appeared right before her bored bleary eyes. She rubbed them to be sure she wasn't seeing things. But the sight was no mirage. Two parking spots down from hers was a gargantuan, deep-throated, Harley Davidson motorcycle. Nothing unusual about that. What startled her eyes was the gargantuan, deep-throated passenger sharing a ride on the back of this particular Harley Davidson motorcycle.

The driver emerged from the store.

"He rides with you?" she asked through her car window. She glanced at her own vacant driver's side and thought about the one who rode with her day in and day out. He had made a distinct impression on the seat next to hers. He almost never made an impression anywhere else.

"Yep," the motorcycle man said. He never even looked at her. "Everywhere I go."

He buckled a shiny black helmet onto his head, revved the engine, and drove away, he and a big yellow tomcat in a matching helmet leaning into the curve as they rounded a corner and disappeared. What a sight.

---

[1] This flash fiction piece first appeared in the online literary magazine, *f(r)Online: Works of Fiction, Nonfiction, Poetry, and Criticism* (October 2, 2015), published by Tethered by Letters, a literary publisher and resource for writers, available at http://tetheredbyletters.com/out-of-the-ordinary/.

Her husband came out of the store with the milk. He settled himself into his own impression and handed her the plastic grocery sack.

"People annoy me," he said. She heard this from him several times every day and suspected she annoyed him too.

"You'll never believe what I just saw," she said. "That Harley that was parked just over there? The biggest tomcat I have ever seen was riding on the back of that Harley. The driver says the cat goes everywhere with him. Can you imagine our Molly cat doing such a thing?"

Her husband started the engine.

"That cat was even wearing a helmet. Can you believe it?"

"Uh-huh," he said. He didn't look at her. She doubted he was even listening.

He buckled his seatbelt and pulled out of the parking lot.

She glanced over at the man who had surprised her eyes twenty-seven years before and asked her six weeks later to marry him. He had one hand on the steering wheel and the other draped across the back of the car seat. Nothing unusual about that, not one bit, not in twenty-seven years.

She rubbed her eyes again. Then, instead of looking straight ahead in silence like she always did when they drove the usual route home, she shifted, inching out beyond the borders of the well-worn indentation her years of journeying had made in her front passenger seat.

Out of the blue, a desire stirred inside of her. She rolled down her window.

"What are you doing?" her husband asked. He even looked over at her.

She didn't answer but instead she smiled and leaned her head out the window, and for the first time since she could remember felt the wonder of the wind.

Chapter 2

O Taste and See

O taste and see that the Lord is good.

—Psalm 34:8

Gordon is a chef, a culinary artist.[1] His alimentary genius amazes me. I know of no one else who can scrounge around in a kitchen when it has been depleted of its weekly grocery stock and, using odd combinations of leftovers, stale bread, languishing vegetables, and other perishables, concoct a delectable feast.

I asked Gordon several years ago what inspires his desire to cook. His answer sounded to me very much like the language of calling.

"I like knowing that people can come to a restaurant where I am cooking, sit down, be served, and enjoy a meal someone has prepared for them," Gordon said. "I am satisfied with my work when people are satisfied by the food I cook."

Most diners in the bistro where Gordon works never meet Gordon. The holy space where he presides over the restaurant's daily cooking rites is behind the scenes, in the kitchen. But diners experience nourishment and delight because of Gordon's artistry and hard work.

[1] A version of this chapter appeared in Jill Crainshaw, "'O Taste and See': Daily Prayer as Wise, Savoring and Saving Action," *Call to Worship* 47, no. 3 (2014).

Gordon's love for food and cooking was born in his parents' kitchen. To eat at the Callahan's house is to enter into a realm of culinary magic. Both Gordon and his parents season their cooking with radical hospitality and gastronomic imagination. Meals prepared by the Callahans are always worth the wait because the food tastes so good and the conversation and fellowship leading up to and during the meal are so nourishing. And there is always enough for that unexpected guest who drops by at dinner time. I know. I have been that unexpected guest.

Some of the best bites of food I have ever tasted have come from pots stirred by Gordon's or one or the other of his parents' hands. Part of the wonder and mystery of those superlative bites is that they are for the most part singular. Even if the same recipe and ingredients are used again, the taste is never the same twice. Each culinary moment combines unique elements of food, conversation, time, and place. Rare and unrepeatable, each culinary moment reveals its own wisdom about life. Each culinary moment—each bite—is to be savored.

My conversations with Gordon have made me consider a question that I think is central to life and liturgy: What is the difference between tasting and savoring something?[2]

I enjoy cooking, and I relish opportunities to experience culinary excellence. I look forward to sampling unusual foods. Experiencing epicurean delights. Learning how different chefs—both professionally trained and homegrown—create foods that nourish and amaze.

I enjoy tasting foods, and certain flavors particularly appeal to my sense of taste. But to savor a food or a dining experience? To savor,

---

[2] Two works inspired my thoughts for this essay: Kirk Byron James, *Addicted to Hurry: Spiritual Strategies for Slowing Down* (Valley Forge, PA: Judson Press, 2003), and Robert Farrar Capon, *The Supper of the Lamb: A Culinary Entertainment* (New York: Doubleday, 1969). Both authors, in their unique ways, encourage savoring life.

for me, is different from tasting. The word "savor" is derived from the Latin *sapere,* which is related to another Latin word, *sapientia,* or wisdom.[3] To savor is "to have the experience of, to taste or smell with pleasure, to delight in." Savoring something requires a certain amount of patience and perhaps even wisdom.

Take dark chocolate as an example: I love the rich, robust taste of dark chocolate. It is both a delicacy and a comfort food. A perfect partner for after-dinner coffee. But I cannot eat dark chocolate in large quantities. It overwhelms my senses and my stomach. Dark chocolate demands that I savor it, that I linger with its flavor and fragrance.

Savoring eludes most people in a world as fast-paced, frenzied, and frantic as ours. We taste countless things every day, it seems, but rarely do we have (or take) the time to savor those things. To linger with them. To delight in or relish them. To consider with curiosity and care their breadth and depth. This is true for our relationships with food and too often for our relationships with each other and with the world around us.

Yet, researchers and practitioners in a number of fields note that taking time to savor at least some parts of our life is important to personal well-being.[4] Savoring is also important to societal well-being, to the overall health of human communities. People who savor creation cultivate wisdom for caring about creation. People who savor the food that creation provides cultivate wisdom about sustainable food sources and a concern for equitable food accessibility. People who

---

[3] *Merriam-Webster,* s.v. "savor," accessed 4 August 2017, https://www.merriam-webster.com/dictionary/savor.

[4] See F. Bryant and J. Veroff, *Savoring: A New Model of Positive Experience* (Mahwah, NJ: Lawrence Erlbaum Associates, 2007); Rita Nakashima Brock and Rebecca Ann Parker, *Saving Paradise: How Christianity Traded Love of This World for Crucifixion and Empire* (Boston: Beacon Press, 2008), Nook Book; Scott Russell Sanders, *Staying Put: Making a Home in a Restless World* (Boston: Beacon Press, 1993), Nook Book; Barbara Frederickson, "How Does Religion Benefit Health and Well-Being? Are Positive Emotions Active Ingredients?" *Religion and Psychology* 13, no. 3 (2002): 209–13.

savor life seek strategies for improving the health and life of creation and of all humanity.

The Callahans and other culinary artists invite us to savor meals. What is striking about their invitation is its everydayness. Gordon's daily life is the life of a chef. As each day begins, he takes in his hands the stuff of the earth—in his case, local and seasonal vegetables, grains, fruit of the vine—and with skill honed by time and experience peels, chops, boils, marinates, and roasts, cooking up in his kitchen dishes both familiar and brand new. Gordon works each day to nourish bodies and satisfy senses. Gordon's everyday work invites diners in his restaurant to savor meals in all of their many dimensions—aroma, taste, table talk. Even to experience being served in a restaurant is to experience a dimension of savoring.

Enjoying meals with the Callahans and hearing Gordon talk about his calling as a chef have made me think about links between savoring and worship. What if all of us are called to take time each day to savor—to pay attention to the gifts of God's good creation and then to do what we can using the skills we have and the resources in our kitchens to satisfy yearning senses and nourish hungry bodies? What if we are called to savor life and then to serve others so that they can savor life too?

How do we learn the arts of savoring and serving? Perhaps the liturgical discipline of daily prayer can teach us something about both. And perhaps one way we pray daily is by working to savor God's daily gifts, grace, and presence. What if daily prayer practices teach us how to taste and see—how to savor and serve—God's goodness, both at the Eucharistic feast table and at kitchen or restaurant or boardroom tables?

Daily Prayer as Savoring Practice

When she was a child, Ellen could not go to sleep without saying the prayer her mother had taught her:

Now I lay me down to sleep,

I pray the Lord my soul to keep.

If I should die before I wake,

I pray the Lord my soul to take.

Ellen was born in the 1960s. As a five-year-old, she had no idea that the prayer she said with her mother just after turning the lights out at bedtime was written in the eighteenth century. She didn't know that there were alternative verses or versions of the prayer. And she didn't notice the rather daunting theology embedded in the words of the prayer.

All Ellen knew was that climbing into bed, pulling the bedcovers up tight around her neck, holding her Mrs. Beasley doll, and having her mother turn off the light and say this prayer with her made her feel safe for the night. Once Ellen started first grade, the simple rhyme expanded as she began to name people and pets and other things she wanted God to keep safe through the night.

As an adult, Ellen couldn't remember when or where she learned the prayer but maturing into adulthood had not erased the words from her memory. Even at midlife, sometimes when she got into bed at the end of a long day, the words and rhythms of that poem would spring unbidden into her mind. And on most nights, the adult Ellen still offered the names of loved ones and life concerns into the darkness after turning off the lights. Ellen still sought God's presence and care as she fell to sleep. Ellen's childhood nighttime ritual shaped in her body, mind, and soul an enduring prayer practice that lingers with her even now that she is in her fifties.

Rituals shape us and stay with us as we embody them across the years of our lives. Consider baseball players. Some are obsessive about embodying certain actions before they take their turns at bat. Or what about the actions we take to center ourselves before giving a speech or singing a solo or even before going to the dentist? Rituals mark times and places. They provide us with containers for holding emotions and memories. Rituals, especially those we practice regularly, can provide us with meaning-making life rhythms that shape how we see God, ourselves, and the world around us. Daily prayer is such a ritual, one that fosters our capacity to savor life and serve others.

In Christian tradition, the term "daily prayer" refers to the practice of speaking and listening to the word of God each day. Daily prayer is the way people seek God's presence as they traverse their Monday through Saturday life terrains.

Christians have in different times and places gravitated toward varied kinds of daily prayer practices. Some practices—both their content and patterns—are carefully scripted. Versions of these practices can be found in denominational prayer books such as the Episcopal *Book of Common Prayer,* the Roman Catholic *Daily Roman Missal,* the Eastern Orthodox *Synekdemos,* the Presbyterian *Book of Common Worship*, and others. Some traditions follow less formalized prayer patterns, but they nevertheless emphasize the importance of praying daily. Christians across a diverse spectrum of beliefs share in common a conviction that praying daily, routinely, and even multiple times throughout each day is vital to deepening faith and cultivating a sense of personal if not communal well-being.

The Liturgy of the Hours is a historic daily prayer pattern that continues to capture the imaginations of individual Christian believers and faith communities. The earliest form of the Liturgy of the Hours, described by several church fathers in the second and third centuries, included morning and evening prayers as well as prayers at other set times during the day. This prayer pattern emerged out of Jewish practices of reciting prayers throughout each day, often at the third, sixth, and ninth hours, and at midnight. By the end of the sixth century CE, the Liturgy of the Hours, also called the Daily Office or the Divine Office, regularly included seven moments of prayer—

sundown (vespers), night (compline), dawn (lauds), early morning (prime), mid-morning (terce), noon (sext), and afternoon (none).

Benedict, a monk in Italy, is credited with articulating in the fifth century a link between the Liturgy of the Hours and daily work: *Orare est laborare, laborare est orare* (To pray is to work, to work is to pray). Other monastic communities also linked manual work to the rhythms of daily prayer.[5] Nuanced forms of the Liturgy of the Hours emerged over time in Catholicism, especially as different monastic communities developed prayer practices distinctive to their contexts.

Over the course of Christian history, daily prayer forms quite different from the Liturgy of the Hours also emerged. Perhaps most enduring in Protestantism are the Daily Office's major hours, or morning and evening prayers. Morning and evening prayers, again reflecting Jewish roots, are based on Scripture, particularly the psalms, and include prayers, songs, and intercessions crafted for the beginning and the ending of each day.

Prayer meetings, often held on a weekday, became popular forms of communal prayer in American religious practice during the Great Awakenings of the eighteenth and nineteenth centuries. Many congregations today continue to hold midweek prayer services that include Scripture reading and Bible study, singing, and prayer. Also, daily devotional guides published by many different denominations and other groups provide Scripture readings and meditations for each calendar day.

Recent years have seen renewed interest among some Protestant groups in the Daily Office. This renewal includes efforts to reclaim aspects of the Liturgy of the Hours. Many denominations now include

---

[5] Lonni Collins Pratt and Daniel Homan, *Benedict's Way: An Ancient Monk's Insights for a Balanced Life* (Chicago: Loyola Press, 2000); Fred Bahnson (*Soil and Sacrament: A Spiritual Memoir of Food and Faith* [New York: Simon and Schuster, 2013]) describes the time he spent with Trappist monks at Mepkin Abbey in South Carolina experiencing the rhythms of work and prayer in their community.

daily prayer resources in their hymnals or supplemental worship aids. Also, a number of recently formed intentional communities, some-times called "new monastics," include versions of the Daily Office in their corporate practices.

Other daily prayer resources are available online, many of them crafted with contemporary concerns and issues in mind. Examples include Celtic daily prayer from the Northumbria community; A New Zealand Prayer Book, created by New Zealander Anglicans; *The Divine Hours*, a trilogy of prayer guides for the liturgical year com-piled by Phyllis Tickle, a well-known voice within the emerging church movement; and *Common Prayer: A Liturgy for Ordinary Radicals*, a print and web-based collection of morning, midday, evening, and occasional prayers arranged to be used in a yearly cycle.

Common Prayer was developed by Shane Claibourne, Jonathan Wilson-Hartgrove, and Enuma Okoro, leaders within the new monastic movement. The primary audience for *Common Prayer* is evangelical Christians, but the content of each day's prayers is drawn from a range of historical and contemporary cultural and denominational sources. The writers of *Common Prayer* state that "liturgy is soul food" and "offers us another way of seeing the world."[6] A primary purpose of *Common Prayer's* prayer cycle is to interrupt life's usual schedules with God's holy rhythms and to weave together what transcends time with what is most common to human time.[7]

The call of daily prayer was and is to invite believers individually and in community to experience the entirety of their lives as guided by rhythms of praise to the Creator. Daily prayer also cultivates an awareness of how God is present with God's people in both momen-tous and mundane life realities. For example, daily prayer can remind

---

[6] Shane Claiborne, Jonathan Wilson-Hartgrove, and Enuma Okoro, *Common Prayer: A Liturgy for Ordinary Radicals* (Grand Rapids, MI: Zondervan, 2010), 7–8.
[7] Ibid.

us: God is with God's people in the bread on the Eucharistic table *and* in the bread on the supper table. God is with God's people in the grains of the field that *become* the bread at Eucharistic and supper tables. And God is also with God's people in the hands of hourly wage workers who bake the bread that we purchase at our local grocery stores and eat together at Eucharistic and supper tables.

Daily prayer's attentive pauses connect our human comings and goings to the rising and setting of the sun and to the changing of the seasons. Daily prayer's invitation to pause in the midst of our everyday days deepens our recognition of God's persistent diurnal work to create, incarnate, and resurrect. Praying daily—morning and evening and at moments in between—connects all of our senses to the deeper realities present in each moment of life and in every fiber of creation.

In "The Universe as Cosmic Liturgy," theologian Thomas Berry offers these insights about the transformative powers of creation's rhythms as humans live and work within those rhythms:

> Each morning we awaken as the sun rises and light spreads over Earth. We rise and go about our day's work. When evening comes and darkness spreads over Earth we cease our work and return to the quiet of home. We may linger awhile enjoying the evening with family or friends. Then we drift off into sleep. . . . As in this day-night sequence, so in seasonal sequence, we experience changes in our ways of being. In autumn our children may spend their days in school and we alter our daily regime accordingly. In springtime we may go out more freely into the warmth of sunshine where some of us plant gardens. In summertime we may visit the seashore to find relief from the limitations that winter imposed upon us. In each of these seasons we celebrate festivals that give

human expression to our sense of meaning in the universe
and its sequence of transformations.[8]

Berry's words echo the wisdom of Psalm 104:

> You have made the moon to mark the seasons;
> the sun knows its time for setting.
> You make darkness, and it is night,
> when all the animals of the forest come creeping out.
> The young lions roar for their prey,
> seeking their food from God.
> When the sun rises, they withdraw
> and lie down in their dens.
> People go out to their work
> and to their labour until the evening. (Ps 104:19-23)

Both Berry's and the psalmist's insights alert us to the universe's
cosmic liturgy and humanity's part in that liturgy.

What is the promise of this cosmic liturgy? Whether we work
through long nights as nocturnal hospital or factory laborers or toil
in the fields from sunrise to sunset or clock unpredictable hours for
corporations or spend our wakeful hours caring for house and home—
in whatever work or play occupies our days—God is somehow with
us and God's rhythms somehow sustain us.

The problem, Berry argues, is that people today have become disconnected from the universe's cosmic liturgy and its daily promises of
God's creative presence. Thus, we have replaced habits of gratitude
and thanksgiving with mindless routines that destroy, violate, and
exploit the earth and its people.

---

[8] Thomas Berry, *The Christian Future and the Fate of the Earth* (Maryknoll,
NY: Orbis Books, 2009), 96.

How does daily prayer reconnect us to the universe's cosmic liturgy? How does it shape life-giving dispositions and habits? Daily prayer heightens our awareness of how God is present in all creation and in every aspect of human living. It invites and teaches us to taste, see, and savor God's grace whether we are embodying a Sunday liturgy in a church sanctuary or sitting down at a chaotically littered desk in an office early on Monday morning or mowing the lawn on a Friday afternoon or cleaning the kitchen after a far too late and much too rushed evening meal with weary family members.

As we saw above, "savor" is related to the Latin word for wisdom. Perhaps as daily prayer teaches us to savor life, it also instills in us wisdom.

The primary biblical sources for the kind of wisdom cultivated by daily prayer are wisdom writings within the Old Testament. The best known of these are Proverbs, Job, Ecclesiastes, and what are called wisdom Psalms. Wisdom writings are also found in Deuterocanonical sources, the Wisdom of Solomon and Sirach. [9]

A goal common to the ancient writers who penned these texts was to shape the characters of persons in their communities so that they would have "eyes to see and ears to hear" (Prov 20:12) God's presence in their everyday lives. They also wanted to cultivate in people the insight necessary for making ethical choices that would lead to communal and personal well-being. [10]

---

[9] "Deuterocanonical" refers to writings that are deemed by some traditions to be part of the Old Testament. Deuterocanonical sources are considered canonical by Roman Catholic and Eastern Orthodox Christians. Most Protestants do not consider them to be canonical. Deuterocanonical sources are included under a separate heading in a number of versions of the Bible. See *Merriam-Webster Online*, s.v., "deuterocanonical," http://www.merriam-webster.com/dictionary /deuterocanonical (accessed December 8, 2013).

[10] William Brown, *Character in Crisis: A Fresh Approach to the Wisdom Literature of the Old Testament* (Grand Rapids, MI: Eerdmans, 1996), 49.

According to the writer who composed the Wisdom of Solomon in the second or first century BCE, wisdom "pervades and permeates all things" (Wis 7:24). This writer places a prayer for wisdom on King Solomon's lips:

> to know the structure of the world and the activity of
>   the elements;
> the beginning and end and middle of times,
> the alternations of the solstices and the changes of
>   the seasons,
> the cycles of the year and the constellations of the stars,
> the natures of animals and the tempers of wild animals,
> the powers of spirits and the thoughts of human beings,
> the varieties of plants and the virtues of roots. (Wis 7:17-20) [11]

Exemplified in this text is a theme shared by many biblical wisdom texts.

God's wisdom, ancient wisdom writers insist, has infused creation from the beginning of time. God founded the earth "by wisdom," established the heavens "by understanding," and broke open the deep "by God's knowledge" (Prov 3:19-20). Ancient sages saw wisdom everywhere—both in the particular skills required to do everyday work (Exod 31:1-6; 35:1-4, 21-19) and in the extravagant and mysterious "work" of the cosmos (Prov 8:22-31), both in the diligence of ants

---

[11] The Wisdom of Solomon (Wis), also called the Book of Wisdom or Wisdom, is thought to have been written in Greek but in the style of Hebrew verse. While the author attributes the book to Solomon, most scholars today argue that it was likely written after the death of Solomon, probably in the second or first century BCE. See David Winston, *The Wisdom of Solomon: A New Translation with Introduction and Commentary* (New York: Doubleday, 1979), and Leo Perdue, *Wisdom Literature: A Theological History* (Louisville: Westminster John Knox Press, 2007).

and badgers (Prov 30:24-28) and in the mythic activities of Behemoth and Leviathan (Job 40). [12]

Even as biblical writers depicted wisdom as a certain kind of knowledge and attitude of heart, they also personified wisdom as a woman. In Hebrew, the word for wisdom is *hokmah*. In Greek, *sophia*. Wisdom/Hokmah/Sophia appear in many biblical wisdom writings as the personification of God's presence. In Proverbs, for example, *Hokmah,* speaks out at the city's entrance gates (Prov 1), traverses urban streets (Prov 8), works beside God to create the world (Prov 8), and sets a feast table in the house she has built (Prov 9). "Pay attention to human life," Hokmah in Proverbs challenges those who pass her in the streets or who travel by her house.

Daily prayer practices strike a similar chord: *Pay attention* to how God is with us in the sights, smells, sounds, and especially stories that we inhabit and live out each day. Pause and give grateful attention to these every day, often earthy things, because they "connect us to vibrant theological truths that dwell *within lived human experiences.*" [13]

By inviting us to pause and pay attention to the sacramentality of all life, daily prayer calls us to the wisdom work of savoring life. It evokes within us an appetite for life and invites from us a commitment to sustaining life and to making the delights of life available to all people. Perhaps daily prayer can teach us how to be at home in the universe, sunset to sunrise to sunset, in a wisely reflective way that renews and redeems the earth and its peoples.

[12] For a discussion of wisdom and work in Exodus, see Ellen F. Davis, *Scripture, Culture, and Agriculture—An Agrarian Reading of the Bible* (New York: Cambridge University Press, 2008), 139–54.

[13] Jill Crainshaw, "Wording Wisdom: The Wise, Strange, and Holy Work of Worship," *Proceedings of the North American Academy of Liturgy* 3–13, *Academic Search Complete*, EBSCO*host* (accessed December 8, 2013).

Daily Prayer as Saving Action

Liturgical theologian Lawrence Hull Stookey writes that "to be deeply Christian is to know and live out the conviction that the whole human family dwells at the intersection of time and eternity." [14] Where do time and eternity touch? Time and eternity touch in those moments and places where God has made God's home with humanity.

That is one of the most profound gifts of the Gospel story. God's Word—God's Wisdom—was with God at the beginning of time (Gen 1, Prov 8:1, John 1:1). Then, in the midst of time, God's Word—God's Wisdom—became flesh and lived among God's people (John 1:14). [15] God—Wisdom and Word—dwelt upon the earth in the person of Jesus. Jesus' body was nourished by the gifts of seed, soil, and rain. Jesus' feet stirred up dust on city streets. Jesus ate and drank. Jesus felt rain fall on his face and squinted his eyes on sunny days. Jesus lived here, on the earth, and so do we.

The practices of daily prayer can stir within us wonder and awe at the fact that we, like Jesus, dwell here on God's benevolent earth. We, like Jesus, are part of God's life-sustaining creation. We eat and drink. We feel rain and sun on our faces. Our bodies are nourished

---

[14] Lawrence Hull Stookey, *Calendar: Christ's Time in the Church* (Nashville: Abingdon Press, 1996), 2.

[15] A number of scholars link *logos* in John with "wisdom" in Hebrew and Greek sources. Rita Nakashima Brock and Rebecca Ann Parker (*Saving Paradise*, 49) write that "in the Septuagint, the Hebrew feminine noun *Hokmah* (Wisdom) in Proverbs became *Sophia* (Wisdom), which was linked to Word, as the principle of creation." This link between logos and Wisdom emerges in the first chapter of the Gospel of John. See also Raymond E. Brown, *The Anchor Bible: The Gospel According to John* (Garden City, NY: Doubleday, 1964), cxxv; Elizabeth Johnson, *She Who Is* (New York: Crossroads, 2002); Sheri D. Kling, "Wisdom became flesh: An analysis of the prologue to the Gospel of John," *Currents in Theology and Mission* 40, no. 3: 179–87, *ATLA Serials, Religion Collection*, EBSCO*host* (accessed December 8, 2013); Sharon Ringe, *Wisdom's Friends: Community and Christology in the Fourth Gospel* (Louisville: Westminster John Knox Press, 1999), web (accessed December 8, 2013).

by the fruits of the earth. Indeed, God's good creation daily saves us by providing for our physical needs and offering to us sensual and spiritual delights.

When we give prayerful attention to the rhythms of the earth—sunset into night, night breaking into dawn, morning giving way to noon and afternoon, and afternoon drawing us toward yet again another sunset—we are reminded: God continues to dwell *with* us here on this earth, our home. God is incarnate *in* us, in our lives. God is at home with us in the neighborhoods and cities where we laugh and play, worship and work, lament and celebrate. God is saving—redeeming—us every day.

Perhaps that means that the work of daily prayer is, in a sense, saving work, as it shapes in us the desire to follow Jesus' concrete examples of generous love for all people and attentive care for creation. Theologian Rebecca Ann Parker expresses it this way in *A House for Hope: The Promise of Progressive Religion for the Twenty-first Century:*

> To say paradise is accessible here and now is not to say the world is perfect or that we should focus on the good and deny the evil and pain around and within us. The serpent lives in the garden, and paradise is a place of struggle, a place where suffering happens and where destructive systems that harm life have to be resisted. But as the early Christian church understood, here is where the hand of comfort can be extended, the deep breath can be taken, and we can live at home in the world, knowing this is enough.[16]

This knowledge, this wisdom, is fostered as we pray together through each day's hours and minutes. And when we foster this wisdom

---

[16] John A. Buehrens and Rebecca Ann Parker, *A House for Hope: The Promise of Progressive Religion for the Twenty-first Century* (Boston: Beacon Press, 2010), 15, Nook Book.

through prayer, its gifts are birthed in us. We become people who extend hands of care, who with generosity and hospitality serve others so that they, in turn, can savor and serve.

The novelist E. B. White is credited with reflecting in an interview that "if the world were merely seductive, that would be easy. If it were merely challenging, that would be no problem. But I arise in the morning torn between a desire to improve (or save) the world and a desire to enjoy (or savor) the world. This makes it hard to plan the day." [17]

By taking up daily prayer perhaps we can learn how rhythms of saving and savoring dance together in our lives and communities. Indeed, when we pray daily, we learn anew how to savor God's here-and-now gifts of generous grace. We are also challenged to recommit ourselves with each sunset and sunrise to reclaiming, renewing, and even saving God's good earth and to being mindful of and prophetically thankful for the beauty and value of all God's people.

[17] Martha White, ed., *In the Words of E. B. White: Quotations from America's Most Companionable Writers* (Ithaca, NY: Cornell University Press, 2011).

Interlude

Saying Goodbye to the Night

For everything there is a season, and a time for every matter under heaven. . . . God has made everything suitable for its time. I know that there is nothing better for them than to be happy and enjoy themselves as long as they live.

—from Ecclesiastes

I had an old dog once. He was not always old. He became old as he and I journeyed life together over a decade or so. His name was Deacon.

My friends said Deacon was an apt companion for a liturgical theologian because he was devoted to rituals. Deacon was committed to "the way we do things every day," from getting up at the precise getting-up hour to walking each morning without fail, to eating at the same time every day, to sitting together in our favorite chair at the appropriate time every evening.

As Deacon grew older, he needed more assistance with his last trip outdoors before going to bed. This required a change in our nightly ritual from sending Deacon out the backdoor alone into our fenced yard to suiting him up with harness and leash and walking with him up and down the sidewalk out front. Much to my surprise Deacon embraced with his usual fervor this change of his nighttime ritual act. I was less enthusiastic.

"You're a liturgist," Sheila said when I complained about the new nighttime outings. "Can't you turn this into a meaningful ritual? Maybe you can think of it as saying goodbye to the night. Don't you liturgical theologians love that sort of thing?"

Sheila had a point, and I began to consider how Deacon was teaching me to pay attention to the night. As I became more intentional about saying goodbye to the night, a new orientation to God's presence seeped into my bones and recalibrated how I embraced the final hours of each day. Over time as Deacon and I wandered up and down our neighborhood sidewalks I began to reflect on the happenings of the day as I looked up into the expanse of a sometimes clear, sometimes muted, night sky, and in spite of myself I began to experience wonder in my heart and in the soles of my feet—in the marrow of my bones.

A nighttime goodbye chant began to emerge as autumn gave way to winter and our walks continued. I was surprised that as the chant emerged from the womb of the evening, its arc stretched from sunrise to sunset and across the human and canine life span to praise and petition an unexpected divine companion—a Holy Other—who met us each night to walk alongside us. A ritual devised to meet the needs of an aging dog had become a sacred prayer discipline. Deacon and I were embodying compline.

Liturgical theologian James K. A. Smith cites the following by the character Keats in *Bright Star*, a film about poet John Keats:

> A poem needs understanding through the senses. . . . The point of diving in a lake is not immediately to swim to the shore but to be *in* the lake, to luxuriate in the sensation of water. You do not work the lake out. It is an experience beyond thought. Poetry soothes and emboldens the soul to accept mystery.[1]

---

[1] James K. A. Smith, *Imagining the Kingdom: How Worship Works* (Grand Rapids, MI: Baker Academic, 2013), 47.

The same might be said of daily rituals like saying goodbye to the night that emerge because of some practical need in our life. These rituals, like diving into a lake, are experiences beyond thought. These rituals, like poetry, have the potential to embolden us to embrace, even to incarnate in our very bones, mystery.

Nuclear physicist, theologian, and astronomy professor Paul Wallace writes that when we look up into the skies on a clear night, we can see about three thousand stars. Then he startles his readers by noting "that if we were to remove our home planet from under our feet we would see 3000 more" stars beneath us.[2] My nighttime ritual with Deacon confirmed for me Wallace's insight. The cosmos holds more life than we can fathom. But here and there, now and then, we can feel in our bones with wonder what eludes our eyes and imaginations.

Something sacramental happened through that undesired nighttime ritual that shaped my way of being in the world. This is the potential of rituals that both in intentional and unintentional ways become sacred liturgies of a sort; acquired habits can and do shape our dispositions toward and actions in the world. Saying goodbye to the night became for me a way to be *in* the night and, if but for a moment, to dwell in the cosmic mystery I felt all around me and beneath my feet.

When the sun lifts its head in the eastern sky,
And the birds begin to sing,
We give thanks, O God, for the dawning light,
And the symphony of hope it brings.

---

[2] Paul Wallace, *Stars Beneath Us: Finding God in the Evolving Cosmos* (Philadelphia: Augsburg Fortress Press, 2016), vii.

Fill my feet with the joy of the morning.
Tune each tendon to the sounds of your grace.
Let each step I take through the streets of the city
Be a note in this hymn of praise.

When we say our farewells to another day,
And the stars begin to shine,
We give thanks, O God, for the moon at night,
And its promises of rest sublime.

Fill my dreams with the hopes of tomorrow.
Lay me down to sleep and give my soul your peace.
Restore my hands; bless my feet; calm my restless thoughts.
May the worries of the day begin to cease.

When age takes its toll on my body
And my hands become feeble and frail,
I will lift them up to give thanks to you
And I'll pray for the strength to sail

Over the river Jordan
Under your stars and your light.
Please guide my boat to the other shore
As I say goodbye to the night.

Chapter 3

Tables in Wilderness Places

Can God spread a table in the wilderness?

—Psalm 78:19

"How can God feed these people with bread in the wilderness?"

—Mark 8:4

When I was a child, I loved Communion Sundays at our Lutheran church out in the country. We were an every-Sunday churchgoing family. My dad and I sat each week in the back pew with Mrs. Overcash while my mom took her place on the organ bench. Craning my neck and sometimes even standing up on the pew to see over the heads of the worshipers in front of us, I watched in fascination as at a certain point in the service every fourth Sunday our pastor did mysterious things with tiny cups of drink and plates of bites of something people would eat a bit later in the service.

None of us in worship had an unimpeded view of the pastor's actions in those moments. In my childhood church, Holy Communion was served from an altar table that was against the front wall. While we sang a hymn, our pastor turned his back to us as he uncovered silver serving plates and took the lid off of a stack of trays that held miniature cups. All I could see from my spot on the back pew was the pastor's hands moving as he took white napkins from the plates, folded them up in slow motion, and laid them aside. I could tell that whatever he was doing was important because he did it with a reverent flourish; actions at the Communion table were holy actions.

What happened in the service after our pastor prepared the altar table was my second favorite part of Sunday worship. Row by row people filed out of their pews into the side aisles and made their way to the front of the sanctuary where in groups of fifteen or so they formed a semicircle around the altar table and the pastor. While my view of what was happening was still limited, I could tell that they were eating something from the silver plates and drinking whatever was in the tiny cups. Something about the way each person's head tipped back to drink that mysterious drink enthralled me.

But the thing I most loved about Communion as a five-year-old was what I experienced when my dad returned to his seat after taking his turn in the semicircle. I knew that in our church children couldn't take Communion until they had been in a special class with the pastor and were confirmed. I wouldn't be old enough for confirmation class until I was in the sixth grade. Until then, my dad and Mrs. Overcash took turns sitting with me in our pew while each of them went to the front. My dad was always the tallest one in his group, so it was easy to see him as he ate and drank. I remember anticipating his return to our pew, waiting for my whiff of Communion. Yes, my dad smelled different after eating and drinking from that tiny cup, and that was my favorite part of Sunday worship. What made Communion holy for me until I was old enough to eat and drink for myself was that smell my dad carried back with him from up front.

I knew as a child watching from the back pew as people ate with the pastor that what happened in church on the fourth Sundays was connected to the Bible. We talked about Communion and the story of Jesus' Last Supper with his friends in my Sunday School class. Our teacher explained that the words the pastor said every month just before people went forward to eat and drink together were the same words Jesus said at that last meal. Even as a five-year-old, squirming and straining to see from the back row, I had the sense that the meal in the Bible story, the heads tipping back, and the transformed aroma of my dad were central to what happened in our church's worship.

I was wonderstruck in my youth by the mystery of those fourth-Sunday experiences, and I remember looking forward to the day when I could eat and drink and smell different. I remember being a little terrified by the prospect too, though I was unsure as to why.

In the Breaking of the Bread

Many people carry childhood memories of Holy Communion with them into their adult experiences of faith. These memories are no doubt as diverse as the traditions that birthed them and the people who experienced them. And yet, what these traditions and many of the childhood memories share in common are biblical food stories.

The biblical story most people associate with Holy Communion is the story of Jesus' last meal with his disciples, a story told in all four Gospels and retold by Paul in 1 Corinthians. Portions of Jesus' words from that final meal, referred to as the "words of institution," have been repeated as a part of Holy Communion celebrations throughout history and across Christian communities:

> For I received from the Lord what I also delivered to you, that the Lord Jesus on the night when he was betrayed took bread, and when he had given thanks, he broke it, and said, "This is my body which is for you. Do this in remembrance of me." In the same way also he took the cup, after supper, saying, "This cup is the new covenant in my blood. Do this, as often as you drink it, in remembrance of me." For as often as you eat this bread and drink the cup, you proclaim the Lord's death until he comes. (1 Cor 11:23-26 [NRSV])

Most ministers speak a version of these words just prior to or as they break the bread and pour the wine or grape juice into the holy cup in Holy Communion services.

Perhaps less well-known to some worshipers are the links between Holy Communion and other biblical food stories. Most scholars agree that the roots of Holy Communion are to be found not only in the stories of Jesus' last meal with the disciples but also in (1) Jewish meal rituals, elements of which are described in Old Testament stories and find their way into New Testament meal stories, (2) meals the Gospel writers tell us Jesus ate with all kinds of people, and (3) meals that are part of biblical stories about Jesus' resurrection.

Striking about the meal stories in each of these groups is that most of them are stories about actual hunger-satisfying meals. In these stories, people gather at meal tables or in wildernesses or on hillsides or beside the lakeshore to share food that comes from the earth and that is prepared by the hands of local bakers and cooks. While churchly interpretations of these stories emphasize their theological and spiritual meaning and value, the meals in these stories, including the story of Jesus' last meal with his disciples, also provide physical nourishment. And in most cases, the meals include fellowship (sometimes harmonious and other times contentious) amongst the diners. As people eat and drink together, stories are shared, meal etiquette observed, and relationships forged.

An example of this is the meal story in Luke 24. This story is familiar for many worshipers because it appears in the lectionary each year during the Easter season. In this story, two of Jesus' followers are traveling from Jerusalem to a village called Emmaus not long after Jesus' crucifixion. A stranger joins the disciples on the road, and the three of them discuss all that has been happening in Jerusalem—Jesus' violent death at the hands of religious and political leaders and the outlandish reports that Jesus is now alive.

When they arrive in Emmaus, the two followers invite the stranger to join them for dinner. The invitation is an offer of thirst-quenching, hunger-satisfying hospitality. What happens as they all sit at the table sharing supper exemplifies the peculiar intermingling of generous hospitality, earthy intimacy, and cosmic mystery that awed me about Holy Communion as a child. The writer of Luke captures the scene in lyrical and memorable fashion: "When he was at table with them, he took bread, blessed it and broke it, and gave it to them. Then their eyes were opened and they recognized him" (Luke 24:30-31).

In the way the Gospel writer tells the story, the stranger from the road who joins the disciples at their table uses familiar meal time gestures (taking, blessing, breaking, and giving bread) that spark recognition. The writer is not clear about why those followers didn't recognize Jesus before this, though we can wager guesses. Perhaps they were overcome by grief, so convinced that Jesus was gone they could not see in the face of the stranger the face of Jesus. Or maybe the resurrected Jesus looked altogether different than he had before his death; maybe the resurrected Jesus was strange in appearance, his familiar essence or that certain look in his eyes or maybe even a certain smell becoming recognizable to them only as they shared together an everyday ritual that had been a regular part of their lives with Jesus before he died.

Or perhaps as they sat at that table and told stories as people do at meal tables, they were surprised to find themselves remembering Jesus in the way that he had told them to at that last meal together:

> Then he took a loaf of bread, and when he had given thanks,
> he broke it and gave it to them, saying, "This is my body, which
> is given for you. Do this in remembrance of me." (Luke 22:19)

Perhaps something in the way the stranger's hands held and broke the bread reminded them of that way Jesus had of breaking bread or the way he broke bread on that last night they ate together before he died.[1] After all, Jesus had broken bread at meal tables in other times and places. Maybe they had been with him for some of those other meals or for that last meal. Whatever the reason, when the stranger broke the bread at that table in Emmaus, the followers "recognized him" (Luke 24:35).

But the story does not end with the unexpected recognition. Consider the story's inconclusive and mysterious ending. No sooner do the followers in Emmaus recognize the stranger than he "vanishes from their sight" (24:31). Had their eyes been playing tricks on them? Was the stranger an apparition? Or had they really seen Jesus? We are left to wonder.

The Emmaus followers must have wondered too, because even though it was evening and the road was likely to be dangerous at nightfall, they rushed back to Jerusalem to report what had happened. Luke lets us listen in on a portion of the conversation they have with the other disciples: "They were saying, 'The Lord has risen indeed, and he has appeared to Simon!' Then they told what had happened on the road, and how he had been made known to them in the breaking of the bread" (24:34-35).

We can almost imagine the rest of what those disciples from Emmaus said or were thinking: "You won't believe what happened. We invited this stranger we met on the road to have dinner with us. He seemed nice enough and was alone. We thought it was the right

---

[1] B. Ward Powers (*First Corinthians: An Exegetical and Explanatory Commentary: A Somewhat Traditional Interpretation Plus Contemporary Application* [Eugene, OR: Wipf and Stock, 2009], 235–36) explores how after Jesus' resurrection and ascension (as narrated in Scripture and observed in Christian history and tradition), early Christian communities' common meals would become a "conscious remembrance of the meals they had shared with the Lord during his physical presence with them."

thing to do to have him stay awhile. But then—well, it all happened so fast, but as soon as that stranger took the bread in his hands, I saw the similarity. That stranger was the spitting image of Jesus. The way he blessed the bread and broke it? He could have been Jesus. But then he was just gone."

The intrigue of the story's benedictory moment intensifies when Jesus materializes in their midst in Jerusalem while they are talking about what had happened. The Luke storyteller captures the disciples' astonishment and startled awe: "While in their joy they were disbelieving and still wondering, he said to them, 'Have you anything here to eat?' They gave him a piece of broiled fish, and he took it and ate in their presence" (24:41-42). In Luke 24, the physical acts of breaking bread and eating fish resurrect for the disciples the presence of Jesus, the one they had seen die.

What the Body Knows

The two food stories in Luke 24 are at once cosmic and earthy. The pairing of the two intrigues me, sparks my imagination, and connects me across years, cultures, and geographies to first-century Christians. Also, when I hear the Luke 24 meal stories read in worship today, I am reminded of the theological and spiritual power of both meals and stories.

First, the Emmaus bread-breaking story reminds me of the capacity of meals—the food, gestures, and conversations that comprise them—to open diners up to expansive worlds and to experiences of divine presence and mystery. Food ingredients, cultural food practices and beliefs, and communal meal traditions intermingle in individual dishes and their recipes and in whole meal experiences to birth distinctive knowledge about human life. Some of this knowledge is spiritual or theological knowledge.

Philosopher and self-proclaimed food adventurer Lisa Heldke writes about the ways the body "knows" through actions of growing, cooking, and eating food:

> The knowing involved in making a cake is "contained" not simply "in my head" but in my hands, my wrists, my eyes and nose as well. The phrase "bodily knowledge" is not a metaphor. It is an acknowledgement of the fact that I *know* things literally with my body, that I, "as" my hands, know when the bread dough is sufficiently kneaded, and I "as" my nose knows when the pie is done. [2]

Something similar could be said about planting, cultivating, and harvesting green beans, tomatoes, and okra. Or about pruning grape vines to encourage healthier and more abundant growth. A peculiar kind of knowing dwells in the hands, wrists, feet, and eyes of the farmer who can tell by how a pea pod feels to her fingers if the time for harvest is near. A unique kind of wisdom has been cultivated in the nose of the grape grower who can tell by sniffing what kind of grapes were used to make the wine that sparkles in the glass at dinner. Farmers and vinedressers know things by touch, taste, and smell—with, through, and in their bodies.

So do cooks, bakers, and food servers. A wisdom both earthy and cosmic dwelt in the bread-breaking hands of the Emmaus stranger, and those dining with him glimpsed in his hands something recognizable and familiar. Perhaps a dimension of that earthy-cosmic wisdom also lived in the hands of the one who baked the bread they ate that night, though Luke, like many of our Holy Communion liturgies, does not include the bread baker in the storytelling.

[2] Lisa M. Heldke, "Foodmaking as a Thoughtful Practice," in *Cooking, Eating, Thinking: Transformative Philosophies of Food,* ed. Deane W. Curtin and Lisa M. Heldke (Bloomington: Indiana University Press, 1992), 203–29, 218.

The body wisdom generated when we grow, cook, serve, and eat food is too often overlooked or unacknowledged in our celebrations of Holy Communion in church. As a child, even before I was allowed to join the semicircle of eating and drinking around the altar table, my nose and eyes and ears knew something about that meal and about divine presence. A wisdom about God—not a metaphorical wisdom only but also a concrete wisdom—even then lived in my body, a wisdom unique to me and my evolving human story and a wisdom vital to the ongoing story of that local church and of the emerging story of God with us in today's world.

I have heard others echo this. A friend recalls with wistful longing her childhood memory of Communion in her Baptist congregation. In her church, worshipers remained seated in their pews to receive Communion. Trays with circular openings to hold the thimble-sized glass Communion cups (yes, in her growing-up years, the cups were made of glass and were washed after Communion Sundays to be used again) were passed from one worshiper to another up and down the pews. At the appropriate time, worshipers drank together and then placed the cups in holders fastened to the backs of each pew.

One of my friend's strongest Communion memories is of the clinking sound that echoed throughout the sanctuary as people put their empty cups in those holders. Even though many years have passed and she now worships in a church where Communion practices are different, my friend says that when she hears a similar clinking sound she is transported back to her childhood church and those growing-up Communion celebrations. A certain wisdom was implanted in my friend from childhood that resides even now in her ears, perhaps even in the marrow of her bones.

Another element of body wisdom present at Holy Communion is the wisdom of taste. Much as my childhood nose was wise with the Holy Communion wisdom that physical senses know in unique ways. Smith writes that the food we eat at Holy Communion has to be experienced as more than representational.[3] The bread and wine of Holy Communion meals symbolize or in some way make present the body and blood of Christ but they also do more than that. We chew on, sip, and swallow these sanctified food items, and they taste like something to us, depending on the kind of bread, the variety of wine or grape juice, and whether we drink from individual cups or a common chalice, the surrounding context, and the life story that we are living as we eat and drink them.[4]

This means that for children who have not been instructed in Holy Communion's traditional or theological meanings, wisdom still resides in the *taste* of the Communion bread, a wisdom that is unique and important to faith formation. For example, the grape juice or wine might taste like rain-wet vineyards. Or the bread might taste like the offering of yeast rolls Grandma baked each week in her kitchen. People who learn to make and name these associations between Sunday Holy Communion celebrations and everyday life are more equipped to connect to holy wisdom and divine presence outside the church walls.

Pastor Susan, my nephew Rob's pastor, acknowledged these associations in the way she prepared six-year-old Rob for his first Communion. In Rob's Lutheran (ELCA) church, children can participate in Communion before they are confirmed if they have had instruction from the pastor. Pastor Susan's instruction consisted of baking bread with first-graders in the church kitchen while talking about church and faith and cooking and eating. Pastor Susan, Rob, and a few other children baked bread together on a Saturday and then shared the bread with the rest of the church during Communion on Sunday.

Rob was unable at the time to articulate a detailed or complex theological understanding of Communion, but that was not Pastor

[3] Smith, *Imagining the Kingdom*, 117.

[4] Carolyn Korsmeyer, *Making Sense of Taste: Food and Philosophy* (Ithaca, NY: Cornell University Press, 1999), loc. 3289.

Susan's primary instructional aim. Pastor Susan connected for Rob and the other children what happens in Holy Communion with what they knew with their hands, noses, and mouths as they baked bread together. She then linked that body-wisdom with worship by using the bread the children had baked for Communion that next Sunday.

This experience illustrates one of the gifts of Holy Communion meal rituals. The foods that make up the sacred meal contain in them basic ingredients from the earth mixed together in certain ways to result in bread and wine or grape juice. The foods also open up into broader and deeper worlds of meaning. This is in part because they come from the earth and in part because human hands transform them into edible delights.

The everyday and earthy images that spiral out and swirl around Holy Communion's sacred food elements are poetic and joyful even as they are at times sorrowful:

- farmers harvesting wheat from sun-soaked fields;
- sleepless nights spent worrying about the drought that threatens those same fields the next season;
- Bojangles bakers stirring up biscuits before dawn;
- minimum-wage workers packaging loaves of white wheat to be picked up at the store by mom or dad on the way home from a long day at a corporate office;
- children going to bed at night with hungry stomachs and no certainty that there will be food for breakfast the next morning;
- flour-dusted family recipes for grandma's sourdough bread;
- the remembered taste of a single butter-slathered yeast roll broken and shared on a wedding night;
- grape pickers in Chile earning $4.00/day;
- bread baked with the pastor in the church kitchen and shared with the community in communion on Sunday morning;

- bread riots in Egypt as recent as 2013;
- God planting a garden "in the East, in Eden," and putting *adam* there;
- God sending manna in the wilderness;
- Jesus refusing to turn stones into bread;
- Jesus the bread of life and cup of peace;
- water becoming wine at a wedding feast in Cana;
- the Welch brothers turning wine into grape juice for Holy Communion;
- Jesus taking, blessing, and breaking five loaves that feed a crowd with basketsful leftover.

In any given worship service any or all of these meanings and experiences and countless others can be and are present in eating the bread and drinking from the cup at the Communion table. The expansive promises and possibilities of Holy Communion reside in meanings like these that are both tied to the actual food elements and mysteriously beyond them.

Food philosopher Carolyn Korsmeyer explores this dimension of Holy Communion meals:

> These instances of bread and wine are both food and not food. They are tasted and swallowed, but not for nourishment. The tastes of the bread and when permitted of the wine—for not all churches allow laity to drink of the blood of Christ—occasion reflection of the profoundest sort. The fact that the sacrament is actually taken into the body indicates the most direct participation the mystical reenactment of God's sacrifice, one that the exercise of any sense other than taste might not render so intimate.[5]

---

[5] Ibid. Korsmeyer writes that "taste requires perhaps the most intimate congress with the object of perception, which must enter the mouth, and which

When we take, bless, break, and give bread to each other around the table, God is with us, and sometimes, in ways that defy explanation but that are profoundly intimate, we taste and see God.

Common Meal or Sacred Food Objects?

"But these multiple meanings, experiences, and stories are not present in my church's Communion celebrations," some worshipers might say. And that is true in some cases. In many communities, the representational or symbolic aspects of Sunday's holy meal—that the bread and wine represent or symbolize Jesus' body and blood—are emphasized in prayers, hymns, and words of invitation and institution at the table while the metaphorical, poetic, and physical links between Holy Communion meals and everyday meals or between the Holy Communion food elements and the soil and hands that birth them are neglected or have been lost altogether.

Theologian Nathan Mitchell locates the roots of this lack of connection in the history of Christian Holy Communion practices.[6] At first, early Christian communities emphasized common *meals* when they worshiped together in each other's homes:

> They devoted themselves to the apostles' teaching and fellowship, to the breaking of bread and the prayers. Awe came upon everyone, because many wonders and signs were being done by the apostles. All who believed were together and had all things in common; they would sell their possessions and goods and distribute the proceeds to all, as any had need. Day by day, as they spent much time together in the temple,

---

delivers sensations experienced in the mouth and throat on its way down and through the digestive track."

[6] See Nathan Mitchell, *Cult and Controversy: The Worship of the Eucharist Outside of Mass* (Collegeville, MN: Pueblo Books, 1982).

they broke bread at home and ate their food with glad and
generous hearts. (Acts 2:42-46)

As the disciples and others remembered meals with Jesus and told stories of what Jesus had done and who Jesus had been in their lives, they
began to develop images and words to express an awe-inspiring mystery they did not understand—that Jesus, though dead and buried,
was somehow in their midst in the breaking of the bread. A full meal
shared in community was a sacred occasion for community members
to encounter God's presence in their midst as they remembered times
when they had shared meals with Jesus, or for later generations, as
they remembered the stories of Jesus that had been passed onto them.

By the middle of the first century, Holy Communion practices and
meanings had already begun to change. Paul penned the words of
institution so familiar to many Christian Holy Communion celebrations today in the letter he wrote to the church at Corinth about 53
or 54 CE. By this time, observes Mitchell, communities had already
begun to understand and embody the meal in a way different from
what we see in Acts 2.

In 1 Corinthians 11, Paul reprimands community members in
Corinth who "humiliate those who have nothing" (11:22) by eating
before all have arrived for the meal. In Paul's descriptions of the
abuses and of the meal itself, we see the shift in practice:

> Now in the following instructions I do not commend you,
> because when you come together it is not for the better but
> for the worse. For, to begin with, when you come together
> as a church, I hear that there are divisions among you; and
> to some extent I believe it. Indeed, there have to be factions
> among you, for only so will it become clear who among you
> are genuine. When you come together, it is not really to eat the
> Lord's supper. For when the time comes to eat, each of you
> goes ahead with your own supper, and one goes hungry and

another becomes drunk. What! Do you not have homes to eat
and drink in? Or do you show contempt for the church of God
and humiliate those who have nothing? What should I say to
you? Should I commend you? In this matter I do not commend
you. . . . So then, my brothers and sisters, when you come
together to eat, wait for one another. (1 Cor 11:17-23)

What Paul describes in 1 Corinthians 11 is a worship pattern where
a common meal is eaten together followed by the Lord's Supper. As
Mitchell notes, this means that "the actions of blessing bread and
cup no longer frame the complete meal" but instead are a kind of
"sacramental appendix" that Paul refers to as the "Lord's Supper." [7]
Before this, reflecting Jewish meal practices, the "Lord's Supper"—the
sharing of bread and cup—were more fully embedded in an entire
meal sometimes referred to as an agape meal.

Mitchell notes that the shift in the Lord's meal practices suggested
in 1 Corinthians is representative of other similar shifts in New Testament communities:

In the New Testament, there seems to be a shift from eucharist as all or part of a meal to eucharist as an independent rite; from emphasis on the act of community dining to
emphasis on the food itself. . . . By the second century, the
eucharist has become ritually independent of the meal . . .
and the "presence of the Lord" became more directly attached
to the food itself, the ritual elements of bread and wine. [8]

What this means is that over time the bread and wine of Holy Communion came to be viewed less as elements of a common *meal* and
more as sacred *food objects* connected to the presence of Jesus.

---

[7] Mitchell, *Cult and Controversy*, 22. Mitchell relies on the biblical interpretations of Norman Perrin, *Rediscovering the Teaching of Jesus* (New York: Harper
and Row, 1967), 102–7, and Willi Marxsen, *The Beginnings of Christology*, trans.
Paul Achtemeier and Lorenz Nieting (Philadelphia: Fortress Press, 1979), 88–122.

[8] Mitchell, *Cult and Controversy*, 39.

Meal-sharing practices are vital to community formation. Relationships are sparked, forged, and sometimes healed as people eat meals together. At tables—whether kitchen tables, ornate banquet tables, picnic tables in the park, or favorite restaurant tables—people share the happenings of their lives, discuss and debate the news, and pour out with the wine deep feelings associated with romantic love, job losses, personal breakthroughs, and despairs. As the emphasis in worship shifted over those early centuries to a focus on the bread and wine as sacred food objects, Lord's meal practices and understandings became increasingly associated with personal devotion and disconnected from these relational dimensions. More expansive associations of Holy Communion with a common *meal* were neglected and in some cases lost.

When the emphasis in Holy Communion is on bread and wine as sacred food objects, also neglected or overlooked are other organic and place-connected associations such as those between sacramental bread and the daily bread that arrives at our tables after a long and artful process of planting, cultivating, harvesting, milling, and baking. When this happens, worship practices around the Lord's table risk becoming flat because the meal has become disconnected from its earthy and storied root system.

When relational dimensions of meal sharing are neglected at the Lord's table, worshiping communities also risk missing out on the power of the meal to cultivate everyday justice and grace. We risk limiting our experiences of Holy Communion to the Sunday sanctuary when we could be recognizing Jesus in the hands of those who break bread at our everyday tables, in the kneading wisdom of the Biscuitville baker, in work of the fieldworker harvesting grapes at a winery, when we could be embodying Jesus in our own hands as we take up our everyday work. We risk doing in the twenty-first century what Paul scolded the Corinthian church for all those years ago—failing to extend the abundant hospitality of the meal to those on the community's margins.

Theologian Letty Russell says that our capacity to link Holy Communion and everyday meals and meal tables is reignited when faith communities foster what she calls "kitchen table solidarity."[9] Russell wonders what kind of "household of freedom"—what kind of church—can be a sign today of God's promised new creation where God's earth is respected and where the humanity and worth of all people are celebrated.

A particular type of furniture holds the place of honor in Russell's imagined household of freedom—a table:

> A lot of community takes place at a table, and the Christian heritage already has a long tradition related to table community, table sharing, table talk, and the like. . . . The metaphor in [*Church in the Round*] speaks of people gathered around the table and in the world in order to connect faith and life in action/reflection (the round table), work for justice in solidarity with those at the margins of society (the kitchen table), and to welcome everyone as partners in God's world house (the welcome table).[10]

When Russell describes the kitchen table, Rob's communion bread-baking experience in the church kitchen comes to mind for me. Pastor Susan, perhaps without realizing it, linked the bread of Holy Communion—the body of Christ—with kitchen bread baking. Russell might argue that Pastor Susan also opened a door into kitchen table solidarity.

Along with Rob's first Communion experience, Beulah's table also comes to mind for me when I consider the importance of Russell's "kitchen table" image.[11] Beulah's kitchen table. At her table, Beulah

---

[9] Letty Russell, *Church in the Round: Feminist Interpretation of the Church* (Philadelphia: Westminster John Knox Press, 1993), 12.

[10] Ibid.

[11] Jill Crainshaw, "Living the Feast: Liturgical Etiquette for Beulah's Table," *Liturgy* 22 (2007). I first reflected on the spiritual dimensions of Beulah's table in this essay.

served steaming bowls of garden tomatoes and squash to seven growing children. She preserved green beans and memories in wide-mouthed canning jars, lining them up on the table, a nourishing sentry to guard her family through the winter. Beulah rocked little ones to sleep in the chair by the wood-burning cooking stove, the ever-present table holding within reach an equally ever-present glass of sweet iced tea.

Beulah's table was neither fancy nor ornate. Newspapers, boxes of cereal, mail, and cookie-filled Tupperware containers camouflaged the tabletop. But that was what made the table memorable, even prophetic. The table's abundant camouflaging made it welcoming of all kinds of everyday realities. Anyone who spent time at Beulah's table knew food and fellowship, nourishment and grace, were always available there.

This was Beulah's legacy. Even when times were hard, friends were welcomed to Beulah's table. So were strangers. At Beulah's table, bread was broken and stomachs and hearts filled. And in the breaking of the bread—the taste, the sharing, the conversation, the sometimes tears—God made God's presence known. This somewhat unlikely Gospel proclamation of hospitality and hope continues to resonate through Beulah's oldest daughter who now lives in the farmhouse and breaks bread at Beulah's table.

How did Beulah's table become a sacred place simultaneously laden with everyday hospitality, down-to-earth grace, and transcendent hope? What is the connection between Beulah's kitchen table and worship's table?

Beulah answered that question before her death. "My church always welcomed my family," Beulah said. "People there saw us through some hard times, even when they were having hard times of their own. It was like all the times we had Sunday dinner on the ground. There was always enough to go around and some left over. Prayer was the same way. Our pastor stood behind the Communion table. People shared their prayer concerns. Then the pastor prayed. I always felt like the church had more than enough love and faith to go around."

Beulah's table is an earthly and earthy metaphor for the justice making that can happen around worship's meal tables. Beulah's farmhouse kitchen table and worship's Communion table share some characteristics: hospitality, nourishment, fellowship, and God's presence. From the vantage point of both tables, a redeemed world can be seen or at least envisioned.

Beulah's table exemplifies the kitchen-table solidarity Russell advocates. The image of a kitchen table reminds us of our daily needs for food and drink and physical nourishment. We thrive—we survive day to day—because the earth offers to our physical bodies its gifts of fruit and grain, gifts that we eat and drink while laughing, talking, and sometimes even crying together day after day at a kitchen table.

When we open ourselves to its complexity of meanings, the kitchen table also reminds us that too many tables in our world today are too empty. In some parts of the world, a malnourished earth groans from abuse and overuse and lack of care. Some once-fertile fields are now barren. Too many people in our communities face every day the possibility that they will not have enough food for their families.

The need is great. Too many tables today relegate those deemed unacceptable to margins where there is neither abundance nor enough. Too many tables are unsafe places of hurtful words and violent actions. Too many tables reinforce oppressive hierarchies by insisting that some people always wear the garments of servant while others consistently don the vestments of those served.

Jesus modeled radical hospitality when he broke and blessed bread on hillsides or by the sea or in the homes of friends and strangers. When Jesus ate with others, he also embodied God's promises of abundant food for hungry people and abundant hope for those who despair. Jesus' meal table promises were and are for spiritual *and* physical nourishment. They were and are for everyday realities even as they point to future hopes. Empowered and energized by Jesus' meal practices, our Lord's table practices today can and should also model and embody these powerful promises both within communal worship and beyond that at kitchen tables and corporate boardroom tables and in the public square.

From Communion Tables to Kitchen Tables
to Wilderness Tables

What can we do to restore Holy Communion's surplus of meanings in those times and places where worship practices around the table have become disconnected from their earthy and storied root system or where the Lord's table is no longer a place of radical hospitality and justice making?

One strategy we can employ is to make associations between everyday life and churchly life more prominent in our prayers, liturgies, and actions at the Lord's table. Pastor Susan modeled this when she used bread baked by Rob and the other children in a Sunday Holy Communion service. Other ways to emphasize everyday associations include:

- naming in Holy Communion table prayers the farmers, millers, and bakers who make possible the bread at the Lord's table;
- inviting worshipers to recall and even to share in worship or at meals following worship bread-baking stories from their everyday lives;
- exploring in sermons biblical meal stories and linking those stories and meanings to contemporary meal practices and food production challenges and possibilities;
- linking local hunger realities with the Lord's table promises of abundance by asking worshipers to bring to the table along with the bread and wine grocery contributions for a food bank or soup kitchen;
- practicing the Lord's Supper as part of a full common meal and imagining around the meal tables how, as in Luke 24, we

somehow recognize Jesus in our midst when we break bread together;

– encouraging worshipers to remember at their everyday tables— kitchen tables, study tables, and even boardroom tables—Lord's table hospitality and justice-making possibilities.

"Can God spread a table in the wilderness?" the psalmist asks (Ps 78:19). The writer of Mark's Gospel echoes this question: "How can God feed these people with bread in the wilderness?" (8:4). These questions are germane today as worshipers gather around Holy Communion tables and as people in communities across the globe gather around kitchen tables in a world of expanding natural and spiritual wildernesses.

Biblical scholar William P. Brown offers a tenuous "yes" to this question. Ancient psalmists celebrate the life-sustaining gifts of God's creation. They notice and exclaim about what Brown refers to as "God's gracious orientation toward creation":

> God's passion for creation is *naturally* realized. Through natural, "ordinary" means, through nature's wondrous workings, God sustains the panoply of life, enabling each animal and plant, each species and ecosystem, to develop and function according to its capacities and vitalities. [12]

But "life's flourishing has become tenuous." [13] Nature's rhythms have been disrupted by human activity and abuse, and this has made the response to whether and how God can spread a table in the wilderness a tenuous "yes."

---

[12] William P. Brown, *The Seven Pillars of Creation: The Bible, Science, and the Ecology of Wonder* (New York: Oxford University Press, 2010), 158.
[13] Ibid.

But while tenuous, the response is still "yes," a "yes" for which we who depend on God's creation for life have a responsibility.

The epiphanies and gifts of creation are "too wonderful" for humans to comprehend (Prov 30:18-19). The extravagant wonders of creation, of creation's incomprehensible and untamed wildernesses, says Brown, are what unite "the empiricist and the 'contemplator,' the scientist and the believer." [14] Brown's hope is that in a world where wonder is giving way to "soulless science" and narrow theological views of creation, a different wisdom that links faith and science, intelligibility and mystery, in a life-giving, life-preserving partnership can be cultivated.

A related hope is that everyday tables and worship tables can also be linked by a wisdom—a body-mind-spirit knowledge—that is rooted in and generates the kind of communal awe and wonder that inspired biblical writers to depths of faith *and* that motivates the best of today's science. If we can work as communities to restore and renew wonder and awe as our common stance toward God, each other, and the earth, then perhaps we can join God in God's work to spread abundant tables in today's wildernesses.

[14] Ibid., 4. Brown links Anselm's word about theology as "faith seeking understanding" with a view of science as understanding seeking further understanding. When these two views are taken together, he says, then theology and science can learn from each other as in their particular and peculiar ways they grapple with ontological realities that confront us today.

Interlude

Encrypted! A Sermon Preached
on the Occasion of World Communion

He put another parable before them, saying, "The kingdom of heaven is like a grain of mustard seed that a man took and sowed in his field. It is the smallest of all seeds, but when it has grown it is larger than all the garden plants and becomes a tree, so that the birds of the air come and make nests in its branches."

He told them another parable. "The kingdom of heaven is like leaven that a woman took and hid in three measures of flour, till it was all leavened."

All these things Jesus said to the crowds in parables; indeed, he said nothing to them without a parable. This was to fulfill what was spoken by the prophet: "I will open my mouth in parables; I will utter what has been hidden since the foundation of the world."

—Based on Matthew 13:31-35 (ESV)

Stars. They encrypt the night skies with mystery and then steal away into the morning light. Maple trees blaze up with the promises of autumn, and pumpkins remind us of harvest gifts. Yes, autumn's beauty reminds us. Here and there, now and then, Spirit winds stir up life's inscrutable veil and we see. The hands of an artist. The hands of a musician. The hands of God.

Psalm 90 speaks of hands: "Let the beauty of the Lord be upon us and prosper the work of our hands." I hear these words, glimpse creation's grandiloquent mystery, and I wonder. What about my hands? Your hands? Too many hands break and destroy. Too many injure and scar. Whose hands will hold broken hearts with gentleness? Whose hands will paint God's grace on landscapes of despair?

For me, these are the questions of Christian ministry that matter. This is where God's love in Christ meets life's raw realities. How do my hands, our hands, join God in God's justice-doing, beauty-creating, music-making work?

A man took and sowed a mustard seed in a field . . .

Maybe we can smell it. Or perhaps we can see him. We don't often see him. He spends most of his time in the fields. Weary boots caked with mud, arms sun-singed and sinewy . . .

A woman took and hid yeast in three measures of flour . . .

Maybe we can smell it. Bread. Baking. Or perhaps we can see her. We don't often see her. She spends most of her time in the kitchen where the ovens are hot and flour fogs the air.

Matthew tells us why they are here in God's gospel story of new life. Jesus' parables—they proclaim what has been hidden since the foundation of the world.

Something hidden? What hidden thing do we need to see on this World Communion Day?

A women took and hid yeast . . .

They are strong hands. Durable. She is up to her elbows in thirty pounds of flour. A stray wisp of hair falls across her flushed face as she works the dough. No bread machine. Hands and forearms move forward and back, back and forward. Relentless. Fierce somehow. Graceful. She is right there in Matthew 13:33. But I haven't noticed her. The yeast is like the kingdom of heaven, people in the know say. So we can't help but notice heavenly yeast. Isn't the yeast the point of the parable?

Who notices her?

She is there. A eukaryotic microorganism hides her. Yeast hides her. But she is there. It is her hands that hide that microorganism in enough dough to feed 150 people. *Enekrypsen* is the Greek word for her taking and hiding action. Like encryption? She encrypts yeast into the dough's viscous density, and the yeast changes the dough. Infiltrates every part of it. The hidden one hides rising-up power in flour and water and lard. The dough rises. Life rises. Bread rises. Political food. Poor people's food. Our food. Sun-goldened loaves seasoned by the scent of the soil.

A man took and sowed a mustard seed . . .

His hands are strong too, but in a different way. Nimble-strong. Dirt-stained fingerprints. That calloused, fleshy part of his thumb and forefinger familiar with every shift and change in the texture of the soil. He takes a mustard seed. A microorganism of a seed. And hides it. Encrypts it. Never to be found again until—it grows into a garden plant expansive enough for all the birds of the forest to nest in its branches.

A woman took and hid . . .

A man took and sowed . . .

Hidden from the foundation of the world. The word "hands" is not in Matthew 13. But a man took and sowed. Is THAT what we are to see? His fingers sowing into the soil a message of expansive hospitality. A woman took and hid. Is THAT what we are to see? Her fingers hiding in that bread the leavening of a radical message: the kingdom of heaven begins with hidden hands. Fragile hands we don't expect too much of. Knobbed and knotty hands we cringe to see. Labor-roughened hands we don't even notice. His hands sowing promises of "home" for all. God's hands—Jesus' hands—creating a home for all. Her hands—shaping the bread of life. God's hands—Jesus' hands—offering the bread of life. Is it possible—in the hands of God's invisible people, we catch sight of God's reign? I wonder.

And what about our hands?

We live in peculiar times. Almost everything we Google or see in the news—so much of what we know and what we think we know is encrypted. Encoded. Full of hidden agendas. I encourage us. Let us seek wisdom for all that remains unsettled in our hearts and minds about life's mysteries. We can search. Study. Pray. Ponder. Get a decoder ring.

But then—God calls us to roll up our sleeves. To plant tiny seeds and have faith in abundant growth. God calls us to get up to our elbows in life's and ministry's sticky dough. Work—forward and back, back and forward. Have faith in all that Jesus promises in these stories and in the radical love Jesus lived out. And believe that the work we are called to do will, here and there, now and then, sow grace into a beaten down world aching to rise again to new life.

We gather today to celebrate World Communion. Communities across the globe are breaking bread today and imagining a world where bread is available and abundant for all people. Even as we imagine a bread-rich world of enough for all, I invite us to look around this community and give thanks for the hands that do God's work right here. Gentle hands that have put "Hello Kitty" Band-Aids on skinned knees. Arthritic hands that knit or build or garden through pain. Large hands that have held tiny hands as first steps were taken. Hands that set music free from pianos or organs or guitars. Hands that calm with a touch or write with a flair or feed with a fierce desire that none will go hungry. This is what we share with other Christians across the globe on this day—God blesses our hands and calls us to use our hands to care for and serve and love others.

Remember: a man took and sowed a seed; a woman took and hid some yeast. THAT just might be what has been hidden since the foundation of the world. God's reign—God's justice—God's good grace and love for all people lives and grows right here—in my hands and your hands, and in the hands of God's people in this city and throughout the world. ALL of our hands hold God's grace: all of our hands are the hands of God.

Chapter 4

Wherever the River Goes

> Wherever the river goes, every living creature that swarms will live, and there will be very many fish, once these waters reach there. It will become fresh; and everything will live where the river goes.
>
> —Ezekiel 47:9

The giggling found me before I found the children. One stood barefoot on the creek bank. The other waded ankle deep in sun-warmed water, holding a crooked fishing pole—a fishing *pole*, not a fish-master aluminum alloy rod and reel. A fishing pole.

"Catch any?" I asked.

"This big," the youngest said, holding her hands about five inches apart.

"No, *this* big," said the other child as he stretched his hands wider than his friend's.

Both children giggled, their grammar of astonished delight becoming one with the gurgling water. As I walked on down the path and saw some tires and other trash in the shallows, I wondered: Are these waters clean? Are the fish they are catching safe to eat?

What do those two children standing ankle deep in trash-littered waters have to do with who we are and what we say we believe as Christian communities of faith?

We can stretch this question out to broader theological proportions: What is Christianity's role today in a world—for an earth—that faces heartbreaking and terrifying dangers from neglect and abuse, climate change, pollution, decreasing water supplies, and other environmental challenges? What is incarnation and how is God working to save us? How do we ground our faith so that our human actions as Christians are actions that lead to flourishing in our cities and neighborhoods?

My colleague Stuart, a Presbyterian pastor, leads workshops that encourage ministry students and faith communities to explore relationships between faith and the water that sustains everyday human life. He often begins the workshops with this question: What stories or images come to mind when you imagine your life story in terms of water? [1]

Workshop participants narrate diverse stories. Some recall joyful times spent with family and friends at rivers or lakes or oceans. Others like to tell fishing tales. Almost always, someone in attendance recalls a story about a time when she or he was awed by the immense power of water that surged up in a storm or a raging river or a flood.

Stuart is wise to begin his workshops about clean water, water preservation, and faith by calling forth participants' personal water stories. The kind of storytelling his question ignites taps into a reality that unites us as individuals and communities: water is a very present part of all human and communal life. As Stuart says, "A river runs through us." A river—water—runs through our communal life, our family lives and stories, our national and global histories, and our physical bodies.

A river also runs through our faith stories. Water is a powerful religious symbol. In Genesis, God's Spirit dances over chaotic waters to stir up and give birth to the wonders of creation. Isaiah promises that God's people will be like well-watered gardens, like springs whose

---

[1] Stuart Taylor, "Class Presentation on Water and Theology," Elkin Presbyterian Church, Elkin, NC, April 9, 2016, workshop.

waters never fail. In the New Testament, Jesus is baptized in the waters of the Jordan River, and in Revelation, a river of the water of life flows clear as crystal. Water, in particular the water of Christian baptisms, symbolizes new life in Christ, the one who is called Living Water in the New Testament. Water in Christian life and practice symbolizes the thirst-quenching, cleansing, and renewing of souls and lives by the creative and redeeming presence of God in Christ.[2]

But water is not plentiful in all places and in some places, waters flow less abundantly than ever before. Also, many people lack access to clean water for bathing, drinking, and cooking. The following statistics from UN Water, a United Nations Interagency on Freshwater Issues, only begin to illustrate the contemporary water crisis:

- Water resources are under pressure, with scarcity affecting around 40 percent of the global populations (CAWMA, 2007);
- An estimated 663 million people lack ready access to improved sources of drinking water (WHO/UNICEF 2015);
- Between 2011 and 2050, the world population is expected to increase 33 percent, growing from 7 billion to 9.3 billion (UN DESA, 2011), and food demand will rise by 70 percent in the same period (Bruinsma, 2009);
- About three-quarters of households in sub-Saharan Africa fetch water from a source away from their home (WHO/UNICEF 2012), and 50 to 85 percent of the time, women are responsible for this task (ILO/WGF, n.d.);
- Agriculture accounts for roughly 70 percent of freshwater withdrawals globally and for over 90 percent in the majority of the least developed countries (LDCs) (FAO, 2011). Without improved

---

[2] Two excellent resources explore links between baptism and ecology: Timothy H. Robinson, "Sanctified Waters: Toward a Baptismal Ethic of Creation Care," *Leaven* 21 (2013): 159–65; Benjamin Stewart, *A Watered Garden: Christian Worship and Earth's Ecology* (Philadelphia: Fortress Press, 2014).

efficiency measures, agricultural water consumption is expected
to increase by about 20 percent globally by 2050 (WWAP, 2012);

- Improving water productivity to close the worldwide gap between supply and demand for water will cost the US $50-60
billion annually over the next 20 years.[3]

How are these statistics about actual water resources and issues in
our world connected to what water symbolizes in Christian life and
practice?

This is the question that energizes the work Stuart is doing with his
church in his community in North Carolina. What Stuart seeks to do in
his workshops and in his work as a pastor is to link understandings of
the sacredness of the water in Christian faith to the sacredness of all
water. Stuart also wants to encourage his faith community and others
to get involved in local and global work to sustain and renew the water
sources and systems that nourish physical as well as spiritual life.

Stuart and others in the community are building their water renewal and sustenance work around their belief that

> as a civilization we are at a watershed moment, a crisis, a
> turning point, a crossroads between saving the planet and
> allowing further ecological catastrophe to unfold. We cannot
> save and heal the planet in the abstract. We can only heal the
> planet one watershed at a time.[4]

---

[3] This data comes from a fact sheet provided by UN Water, the United Nations
Interagency Mechanism on all Freshwater Related Issues, including Sanitation.
Resources used to create the fact sheet include Comprehensive Assessment of
Water Management in Agriculture (CAWMA); Food and Agriculture Organization
of the United Nations (FAO), http://www.fao.org/docrep/017/i1688e/i168; Interna-
tional Labor Organization (ILO); United Nations Department of Economic and
Social Affairs (UN DESA); United Nations World Water Assessment Program
(WWAP). See http://www.unwater.org/statistics/en (accessed October 21, 2016).

[4] See http://www.watershednow.com for a description of the work that Stuart
and his First Presbyterian Church congregation, along with a number of local

The "one watershed at a time" emphasis is central to a citywide project, Watershed Now, that Stuart and his church and other city and county leaders have created to encourage residents to be more attentive to and thus better stewards of their watersheds.

A number of community businesses, congregations, civic organizations, and public service groups, including a middle school, are joining forces in Elkin around the Watershed Now project. Their collaborations have included educational workshops, film and lecture series, community-wide water activities on Earth Day and during the local Creek Week, [5] and other activities designed to expand and deepen "watershed awareness." [6] "There are 2,000 watersheds in the US, seventeen in North Carolina," the project website says. "The Yadkin/Pee Dee is the 2nd largest in North Carolina at 7,221miles. The Yadkin is our ecological address. This is our watershed, the basin of life that holds and sustains our life and all of life." [7] The work to renew and restore our earth's water sources—a global undertaking—begins with what Watershed Now refers to as our local "ecological address," with our local dwelling places.

This emphasis on beginning with our own places centers theologian Ched Myers's "watershed discipleship" project. "Watershed discipleship" refers to Myers's work to transform the way Christians in the United States think about and act on water issues related to climate change. Two of Myers's emphases are vital as we seek ways to connect spiritual and baptismal waters to everyday waters.

---

business and community partners, are doing "to support clean water education and awareness"(accessed October 21, 2016).

[5] Creek Week is an annual event held by cities and communities across the United States. Many Creek Week initiatives began with creek and stream cleanup efforts. Programs have now expanded in many places to include collaborations with local schools, creek crawls, creek and stream restoration emphases, and watershed education.

[6] See http://www.watershednow.com (accessed October 21, 2016).

[7] Ibid.

First, Myers sinks the roots of what he calls "a theology of hydration" down into the peculiar and particular soil of each local neighborhood and community. One of the most effective actions we can take to preserve and renew an earth in ecological crisis is to attend first to the parcels of land where we live, work, and play. Many ecological theories and theologies, Myers says, are "too abstract (debating 'new cosmologies'), focused on remote symptoms (tropical rain forests or polar ice caps), or merely cosmetic ('greening' congregations through light bulb changes while avoiding controversies such as the Keystone XI pipeline)."[8] We need to know the curves and turns, the energies and frailties, of our own watersheds. If we want to restore the earth, we need to begin with our own places.[9]

Second, Myers links watershed discipleship to biblical and theological traditions and sources:

> A watershed paradigm recovers the heart of the biblical tradition while challenging dysfunctional characteristics of industrial civilization. It reasserts the priority of creation over all human ideological and hegemonic claims, recovers incarnation in the face of placeless theological abstractions of modernity, and remembers that the people of God covenanted with specific land as caretakers of the divine gift.[10]

One way Myers's watershed discipleship "recovers incarnation" is by remembering that Jesus was baptized in the Jordan River *watershed*.

The Jordan River is a significant Christian image. When we read biblical accounts of Jesus' baptism or refer to "the Jordan" in hymns, prayers, or liturgies, an expansive symbolic and theological world

---

[8] Ched Myers, "A Watershed Moment," *Sojourners* (May 2014): 21. See also Myers, "From 'Creation Care' to 'Watershed Discipleship': Re-Placing Ecology Theory and Practice," *The Conrad Grebel Review* 32, no. 3 (Fall 2014): 250–75.

[9] Myers, "A Watershed Moment," 21.

[10] Ibid., 22.

opens up before us. Consider baptismal liturgies and practices: when we baptize in our local congregations, we remember biblical stories of Jesus' baptism and proclaim that in our baptisms we are "buried and raised again to new life" (Rom 6:4; Col 2:12) like Jesus was in his baptism in the Jordan River. Embedded in this liturgical baptismal action and pronouncement are mythic links to the Jordan River as a "river of life" or as "living water."

What Myers invites us to acknowledge is that in addition to being the mythic sacred place of Jesus' baptism, the Jordan River also was and is an actual river in an actual bioregion. The Jordan River is part of the geography of the Jordan River watershed that today gives life and threatens life in numerous Middle Eastern regions, including Israel, the West Bank, and Jordan.

Issues surrounding water usage and rights in the Jordan River watershed today are volatile and stand at the center of what some researchers call Middle Eastern hydropolitics. Water needs exceed water supply in most areas of the Jordan River watershed, resulting in water wars that escalated in the 1960s and that along with other contentious political issues ignite militarized disputes today. Population and immigration growth continue to contribute to the water deficit in the region. Political and economic conflicts, including the Arab-Israeli and Israeli-Palestinian conflicts, have for many years had connections to the Jordan River water supply.

As many historians and environmentalists as well as political scholars note, the relationship between water resources and politics in the Middle East is complex and burdened by historical, geographical, cultural, religious, and racial tensions.[11] The combined realities of intensifying water crises and water conflicts mean that Middle Eastern

---

[11] Aaron Wolf, "Water for Peace in the Jordan River Watershed," *Natural Resources Journal* (Summer 1993): 797–839.

peace cannot happen apart from cooperative work to preserve, restore, and share the resources of the Jordan River watershed.

These on-the-ground and in-the-water realities of the Jordan River watershed mean that even as Christians celebrate the Jordan River as the place of Jesus' baptism and as a metaphor for the living waters of faith, we must also recognize it as an actual place of political controversy where people live and work, cook and eat, wash their clothes, and water their crops. This gets at a significant point Myers makes through his call to watershed discipleship. All of our baptizing places, like the Jordan River, are supplied by watersheds, many of which are disputed sites or face ecological crisis due to climate change. We incarnate Jesus—we are disciples of Jesus—in actual bioregional locales.[12] This means that the watersheds where we baptize people in and with water in the name of Jesus are also vital sources of our physical and economic well-being.

Myers has titled one of his essays "From 'Creation Care' to 'Watershed Discipleship': Re-Placing Ecological Theory and Practice." The title and content of the essay point to Myers's strategy for reuniting the metaphorical or symbolic with the material or physical in our theologies and spiritual practices. Myers echoes environmentalist Wendell Berry's warnings about the placelessness, isolation, and alienation of many people in contemporary communities and calls for practices of re-placement.[13]

What is re-placement? Myers echoes other environmental activists and eco-theologians when he emphasizes how churches are placed communities. Many people still live within a twenty- to thirty-minute

[12] Kirkpatrick Sale (*Dwellers in the Land: The Bioregional Vision* [University of Georgia Press, 2000]) defines a bioregion as a life-territory governed by the rules of nature rather than by legislative rules—as quoted on the Watershed Discipleship website, http://watersheddiscipleship.org/what-is-a-watershed/.

[13] Myers, "From 'Creation Care' to 'Watershed Discipleship,'" 250–75.

drive of where they worship. To arrive at church, we pass by shopping centers and gas stations, parks and civic buildings, neighborhoods and schools. We live in particular places; we dig our churches' architectural foundations into the ground in particular places; we baptize using the water that flows through pipes to us from the wells or rivers or streams of particular places. To recognize these placed realities is itself an act of worship, even a sacramental act.

The sacramental journey begins, says liturgical theologian Alexander Schmemann,

> when Christians leave their homes and beds. They leave, indeed, their life in this present and concrete world, and whether they have to drive fifteen miles or walk a few blocks, a sacramental act is already taking place, an act which is the very condition of everything else that is to happen. For they are now on their way to constitute the Church, or to be more exact, to be transformed into the Church of God. They have been individuals, some white, some black, some poor, some rich, they have been the "natural" world and a natural community. And now they have been called to "come together in one place," to bring their lives, their very "world" with them and to be more than what they were: a new community with a new life. We are already far beyond the categories of common worship and prayer. The purpose of this "coming together" is not simply to add a religious dimension to the natural community, to make it "better"—more responsible, more Christian. The purpose is to fulfill the Church, and that means to make present the One in whom all things are at their end, and all things are at their beginning.[14]

An important next step in enlivening worshipers' sacramental sense of "their life in this present and concrete world," is to connect (or

---

[14] Alexander Schmemann, *For the Life of the World* (Crestwood, NY: St. Vladmir's Seminary Press, 2004), 27.

reconnect) sacred symbols of our worship to their "bioregional ma-
teriality," in other words, to ignite worshipers' consciousness of their
local places. [15] In terms of water, this means sparking worshipers'
awareness of their local watersheds, their ecological addresses. What
is needed, it seems, is a renewed sense of incarnation as what Katerina
Friesen calls "reinhabitation."[16] We incarnate Jesus wherever we inhabit places. But we inhabit places in sometimes healthy, sometimes
unhealthy, ways.

An unlikely biblical text from Ezekiel has invited me to consider
connections between incarnation and habitation, between faith and
placed-ness, in new ways:

> Then he brought me back to the entrance of the temple; there,
> water was flowing from below the threshold of the temple
> towards the east (for the temple faced east); and the water
> was flowing down from below the south end of the threshold
> of the temple, south of the altar. Then he brought me out
> by way of the north gate, and led me round on the outside
> to the outer gate that faces towards the east; and the water
> was coming out on the south side.
>
> Going on eastwards with a cord in his hand, the man mea-
> sured one thousand cubits, and then led me through the water;
> and it was ankle-deep. Again he measured one thousand, and
> led me through the water; and it was knee-deep. Again he
> measured one thousand, and led me through the water; and

---

[15] Myers, "A Watershed Moment," 24. See also Daniel Kemmis, *Community and the Politics of Place* (Norman: University of Oklahoma Press, 1992); Steven Gregory, *Corona: Race and the Politics of Place in an Urban Community* (Princeton, NJ: Princeton University Press, 1999); Lia Bryant and Jodie George, *Water and Rural Communities: Local Politics, Meaning, and Place* (Routledge, 2016).

[16] Katerina Friesen, "The Great Commission: Watershed Conquest or Watershed Discipleship?" in *Watershed Discipleship: Reinhabiting Bioregional Faith and Practice*, ed. Chad Myers (Eugene, OR: Cascade Books, 2016).

it was up to the waist. Again he measured one thousand, and it was a river that I could not cross, for the water had risen; it was deep enough to swim in, a river that could not be crossed. He said to me, "Mortal, have you seen this?"

Then he led me back along the bank of the river. As I came back, I saw on the bank of the river a great many trees on one side and on the other. He said to me, "This water flows towards the eastern region and goes down into the Arabah; and when it enters the sea, the sea of stagnant waters, the water will become fresh. Wherever the river goes, every living creature that swarms will live, and there will be very many fish, once these waters reach there. It will become fresh; and everything will live where the river goes. People will stand fishing beside the sea from En-gedi to En-eglaim; it will be a place for the spreading of nets; its fish will be of a great many kinds, like the fish of the Great Sea. But its swamps and marshes will not become fresh; they are to be left for salt. On the banks, on both sides of the river, there will grow all kinds of trees for food. Their leaves will not wither nor their fruit fail, but they will bear fresh fruit every month, because the water for them flows from the sanctuary. Their fruit will be for food, and their leaves for healing. (Ezek 47:1-12)

A visiting chapel preacher at Wake Forest University School of Divinity, Delman Coates of Mt. Ennon Baptist Church in Clinton, Maryland, chose Ezekiel 47 for his sermon text for a Tuesday chapel service in November 2015.

I remember thinking as the text was read aloud in the service that day that I could not recall having ever heard those verses before in worship. One reason for this for me as a lectionary-based preacher is that Ezekiel 47 does not appear in the lectionary.

"Who even makes it through forty-seven chapters of Ezekiel?" a friend said later. Church folks might remember and even be enamored with Ezekiel's dry bones (37:1-14) or that peculiar image of the wheel in a wheel (1:15-21), but the rest? Grumpy words from a grumpy exiled prophet.

My friend's words hold truth. Most of Ezekiel amplifies the voice of a prophet who is worked up about the faithlessness and injustice he encounters all around him. We see his righteous indignation in the textures and colors he uses to depict God and in the edgy words he uses to denounce his generation's idolatry. Ezekiel is a disruptive and unpopular sentinel determined to restore his community's attentiveness to the fidelity God expects from them.

Ezekiel speaks harsh words, most of which are not popular subjects for sermons. But in chapel on that day, I was captivated by an invigorating and hope-saturated word picture I heard in Ezekiel. The images sparked my imagination (see Ezek 47:8-12):

Stagnant waters refreshed, dancing, gurgling, singing again,

Swamplands kept wild and salty, noisy with night frogs and snapping turtles,

Lush orchards where trees birth fruit in every season.

Ezekiel 47 promises and celebrates a kaleidoscopic explosion of sweet, nourishing, flourishing, healing fecundity.

Striking about Ezekiel 47's celebration is how through it, Ezekiel shows his ancient community and our contemporary ones something about a grounded theology, a theology that moves with watery flow through and between institutional church life and everyday life. Ezekiel depicts what Christian ethicist Christine Peppard says is the link between theology and hydrology, between theology and how water moves across the earth's lands.[17] Ezekiel portrays "rehydration as

---

[17] Christine Peppard, "Hydrology, Theology, and *Laudato Si,*" *Theological Studies* 77 (June 2016): 416–35. See also Peppard, *Just Water: Theology, Ethics, and the Global Water Crisis* (Maryknoll, NY: Orbis Books, 2014).

redemption" for a time when living waters have become endangered waters. [18]

I wonder. Can we imagine for our spiritually and ecologically drought-stricken places Ezekiel's picture? Can we fathom new life—restored life—in places where ecological realities, agricultural overuse and abuse, and industrial destruction are creating infertile wildernesses?

The call I heard in Ezekiel in the chapel service that day is to churches. I heard Ezekiel calling faith communities to embrace their role in restoring life in times of drought and despair. If everything—cities, valleys, orchards, and swamplands—if everything is going to flourish "wherever the river goes," the water must flow not only into but also out across the "threshold of the temple" (Ezek 47:1), through fields and valleys and into devastated and dying city places. The vision God paints before Ezekiel's wilderness-and-destruction-weary eyes is of a deepening river rushing out *from the temple* and into the city to revolutionize—to heal and redeem—the land and God's people.

Ezekiel's vision is a powerful reminder. Water is more than a religious metaphor.[19] Without water, there is no life—spiritual or physical life.

Consider the most obvious and visual use of actual water in Christian communities—for baptisms. Where do churches today get water for indoor baptisms? In Winston-Salem, North Carolina, where I live, baptismal water is sometimes well water; it comes from groundwater fed by aquifers deep beneath the earth's surface. More often baptismal water is pumped through the city and into church fonts and baptis-

---

[18] Ched Myers, "Re-inhabiting the River of Life (Rev. 22:1-2): Rehydration, Redemption, and Watershed Discipleship," *Misseo Dei: A Journal of Missional Theology and Praxis* 5 (August 2014).

[19] The Anima Series, "Water: More Than a Metaphor; Jon Jorgenson," *YouTube*, August 15, 2014; www.youtube.com/watch?v=V15Lnvf0n_0 (accessed June 7, 2017).

teries from the Yadkin River. A complex public water transportation network, maintained by the city government, snakes beneath paved streets and concrete sidewalks, mostly unseen and unnoticed by residents. On most days, unless a pipe bursts or springs a leak or something goes awry in our water treatment facilities to limit or prevent access to the water in our bathrooms or kitchens or water fountains, we access the abundant, life-giving wetness of the Yadkin River as if by magic through the simple act of turning on a kitchen or bathroom tap.

But water access does not happen by magic. Workers in water and wastewater treatment plants spend twenty-four hours each day monitoring water levels and pressures, water transport infrastructures, water treatment balances, and wastewater treatment procedures. I will never forget the commitment and loyalty I heard in John's voice on the day students from my sacraments and ordinances class and I visited our county's water treatment plant. John works for one of the county's water treatment plants. He recounted with no small measure of pride his confidence in the cleanliness of and unhindered access to "his water" throughout the city and county. John is an expert who does his work with care and skill to make that water magic happen in homes and businesses across the county. On some level, the work is very personal for him, perhaps a kind of calling.

Fortunately, John told us, the Yadkin Pee Dee River Basin is an abundant water source for Forsyth County and twenty-one other North Carolina counties, and that makes his job easier. But the basin faces many challenges to its health, such as expanding urban development, population growth, storm water run-off, and soil erosion.[20] The same is true for other water basins and watersheds across the

---

[20] For more information, see the website for North Carolina Environmental Education, Department of Environmental Quality, Office of Environmental Education and Public Affairs, http://www.eenorthcarolina.org/Documents/River Basin_pdfs/final_web_yadkinpeedee.pdf (accessed October 21, 2016).

United States and around the globe, and as discussed above, in many places water crises are more critical than they are in Forsyth County.

Even in North Carolina in general and in Forsyth County in particular where the water supply at present is abundant, water issues are complex and becoming more prevalent in the courts and in the news. The title of an essay by environmental law expert Richard Whisnant captures a question at the heart of the issue in North Carolina and in other states: "Who Owns the Water?"[21] This question is most pressing for issues involving groundwater in various North Carolina locales.

Conversations and debates about water ownership are complex to begin with, says Whisnant, because of water's mysterious, uncontainable nature:

> Things, like water, that are always moving, often in mysterious ways, and that are so vital to us that we can't imagine life without them, just don't fit well in simple definitions of "property." To make matters especially complicated for water, the law has come to treat its ownership very differently as it moves through the eternal cycle in which it always moves: from ocean to sky, back to earth as rain ("stormwater") or snow, then either infiltrating into the ground (groundwater) or into streams and lakes (surface water), and then passing through myriad human channels, including our own bodies, on its way back to the sea.[22]

Who, indeed, owns boundary-crossing, sometimes raging and storming, sometimes peaceful and calming, water?

Perhaps even more elusive is Whisnant's second question: "Who Owns the Stormwater?"—the water that falls as rain before it makes

[21] Richard Whisnant, "Who Owns the Water? Pt. 1, Groundwater," *Environmental Law in Context*, UNC School of Government, April 20, 2015, http://elinc.sog.unc.edu/who-owns-the-water-pt-1-groundwater/.
[22] Ibid.

its way into soil and our groundwater. And how do we negotiate complex and often contentious legal debates about water in these times when the health and sustainability of our cities' and communities' water is at stake? Discussions of the chaotic legal and environmental issues related to water rights overflow the limits of this chapter, but Whisnant makes a point informative for the questions Christian communities face as they decide how to respond to local and global contemporary water crises.

"Water ownership," he says, "has more in common with ownership of wild animals than with ownership of houses or fiddles" (yes, *fiddles*).[23] Whisnant suggests with this comparison, and he describes throughout his essay, how water moves beneath and above earth's surface in ways that defy all human contrived boundary markers. One result is that water's unruly flow unites and networks people across legal and even national borderlines.

Controversies nevertheless abound: recent years have seen an upsurge in water disputes in North Carolina and surrounding states. In 2015, after a yearslong legal battle, a court of appeals required the city of Asheville to transfer ownership of its water system to regional authorities. In another example, a fight continues in West Virginia to shift ownership of the West Virginia American Water Company from private to public hands. Reasons for this intense battle include the private company's proposed rate increases as well as concerns by some citizen groups that the private company is not prioritizing water safety.[24]

These examples are representative of similar debates and battles continuing and emerging across the United States and in places around the world. Consider this random selection of water-focused

[23] Ibid.
[24] Spencer King and Molly Moore, "Water Rights a Hot Topic in North Carolina, West Virginia," *Appalachian Voices: Protecting the Central and Southern Appalachian Mountain Region,* December 9, 2015, http://appvoices.org/2015/12/09/water-rights/(accessed October 21, 2016).

news headlines: "Why global water shortages pose threat of terror and war" (*The Guardian,* February 2014), "A Thirsty, Violent World" (*The New Yorker,* February 2015), "Water Wars Are Coming" (*PBS News Hour,* November 2015), "Will the World's Next Wars Be Fought over Water?" (*Los Angeles Times,* March 2016). The headlines bespeak grim predictions. As droughts and water shortages expand and people become anxious about having enough water, "desperately thirsty societies take up war against one another." [25]

A troubling contemporary instance of this is the Syrian refugee crisis. Syria experienced one of the worst droughts in history between 2007 and 2010. The twin stressors of drought and political conflict resulted in hundreds of thousands of displaced citizens seeking food, shelter, and water. As *Los Angeles Times* reporter, Peter Engelke writes, combatants in the political conflict "have 'weaponized' water, meaning they have turned it into an instrument of war," at times flooding vulnerable areas and at other times withholding water. [26]

Many displaced Syrians are seeking safety in one of the world's driest countries, Jordan, straining Jordan's already tapped out water resources. A 2013 essay in *Time* by reporter Aryn Baker wonders if Syria's refugee crisis "will drain Jordan of its water." [27] What was reported in 2013 continues to be true about Jordan, which "is one of the most water-stressed countries in the world, subject to ongoing drought that has devastated agricultural prospects in the country's northern regions for decades." [28] Now, many refugees are seeking sanc-

[25] Peter Engelke, "Op Ed: Will the World's Next Wars Be Fought Over Water?" *Los Angeles Times,* March 22, 2016, http://www.latimes.com/world/global -development/op-ed/la-fg-global-water-oped-story.html (accessed October 21, 2016).

[26] Ibid.

[27] Aryn Baker, "Will Syria's Refugee Crisis Drain Jordan of Its Water?" *Time,* April 4, 2013, http://world.time.com/2013/04/04/how-syrias-refugee-crisis-is -draining-jordans-scarce-water-supply/ (accessed October 21, 2016).

[28] Ibid.

tuary elsewhere, expanding the refugee crisis to global proportions as thousands from Syria and other war-torn places risk the dangers of crossing the Mediterranean Sea in unseaworthy vessels to seek asylum in European countries. [29]

Water is powerful—life-giving and life-denying, destructive and cultivating, peaceful and raging—and the power of actual water has intensified water's power as a religious symbol. Even some recent news headlines about water scarcity and water battles utilize religious water metaphors.

An August 2013 USAID online journal headline, for example, brings to mind biblical references: "Water from a Stone: Jordanians Stretch Meager Resources to Sustain Syrian Refugees." [30] Biblical links to the idiom, "water from a stone," appear in the Hebrew Bible in two places—Exodus and Numbers. In Exodus, the Israelites complain to Moses about the lack of water in the wilderness places where they are sojourning. God tells Moses to strike a rock at Horeb. Moses does, and sweet, drinkable water flows from the rock (Exod 17). Numbers recounts an episode when the people complain to Moses and Aaron about the lack of water to drink and food crops to eat. Here, as in Exodus, Moses strikes a rock and water surges from it (Num 20).

Like recent news stories about water, these biblical water tales remind us that even as water is a commanding spiritual symbol and metaphor, it is also a vital physical agent in human life and in the flourishing of communal life. This takes us back to our earlier question:

[29] Rick Noack, "Another Dead Baby Becomes the Latest Heartbreaking Symbol of the Mediterranean Refugee Crisis," *Washington Post,* May 31, 2016, https://www.washingtonpost.com/news/worldviews/wp/2016/05/30/a-dead-baby -becomes-the-latest-heartbreaking-symbol-of-the-mediterranean-refugee-crisis/ (accessed October 16, 2016).

[30] Kathy Sullivan, "Water from a Stone: Jordanians Stretch Meager Resources to Sustain Syrian Refugees," *Frontlines,* July/August 2013, https://www.usaid .gov/news-information/frontlines/aid-action-delivering-results/water-stone -jordanians-stretch-meager (accessed October 21, 2016).

How are actual water resources and issues in our world connected to what water symbolizes in Christian life and practice?

Baptism is a core act of Christian faith and Christian community making. Jesus' baptism in the Jordan and Jesus' later instruction to his first followers to "go and make disciples of all nations, baptizing them in the name of the Father and of the Son and of the Holy Spirit" (Matt 28:16-20) set the stage for water baptism to become a primary Christian identity marker. Even today, after centuries of community-fragmenting water wars over baptism's meaning, theology, and practice, baptism, along with the Lord's Supper, continues to be a central liturgical practice. Most Christians today continue to follow Jesus' example and commission by sprinkling or dipping or dunking or immersing community members in water and announcing age-old biblical promises that "we have been buried with [Jesus] by baptism into death, so that, just as Christ was raised from the dead by the glory of the Father, so we too might walk in newness of life" (Rom 6:4). Christian identity is tied up with—immersed in—water.

Too often forgotten or overlooked is that these profound meanings of baptismal waters are interwoven with the realities of water scarcity and usage in everyday life in neighborhoods and cities not only in biblical places like Jordan and Israel but in each Christian's local dwelling place. Both physical realities and metaphorical meanings of water shape Christian identities in all times and places.

The children fishing along the creek described in this chapter's opening paragraphs illustrate this. What if those creek waters are unsafe? That creek is a stone's throw from my own dwelling place and is a local indicator of worldwide realities. People in our own backyards as well as people in varied places in the United States and throughout the world do not have access to safe water for cooking, drinking, washing, and playing. We need the galvanizing call of Ezekiel's vision.

Two other examples come to mind. Often in the news are the recent coal ash spills and debates in North Carolina. Coal ash, the waste that remains when coal is burned, is usually collected in a dump site called a pond. North Carolina has thirty coal ash ponds. In the last several years, incidents have occurred that draw into question the safety of these ponds for surrounding rivers and streams.

In 2014, a pipe burst under one of the ponds operated by Duke Energy, causing 39,000 tons of the ash to leak, or spill, into the Dan River. This spill was deemed by many scientists, politicians, lawmakers, and others "one of the biggest environmental disasters in our state's history." [31] Debates continue even now, more than two years later, about how toxic substances in the coal ash are impacting water sources, wildlife, and even crops. Politicians, regulators, and Duke Energy officials also continue to wrangle over how to clean up the Dan River and prevent such a spill from happening again. Some people who live near the ponds have complained of contamination in their wells.

Another example is from Flint, Michigan. The water crisis in Flint began as early as June 2012 (and perhaps earlier according to some researchers) and resulted in lead seepage into the city's drinking water.[32] This sparked a major public health crisis that prompted President Obama to declare a federal state of emergency in the city. According to the World Health Organization "Fact Sheet" reviewed in September 2016, high lead levels in human bloodstreams are particularly harmful to women and children and can cause learning and other mental disabilities as well as behavior problems.[33]

---

[31] Jonathan Rodriguez, "NC Coal Ash Spill Cleanup Continues 2 Years Later, *WNCN.com*, February 2, 2016, http://wncn.com/2016/02/02/nc-coal-ash-spill-clean-up-continues-2-years-later/ (accessed October 21, 2016).

[32] For additional information, see Merrit Kennedy, "Lead-Laced Water in Flint: A Step-by-Step Look at the Makings of a Crisis," *NPR*, April 20, 2016, www.npr.org/sections/thetwo-way/2016/04/20/465545378/lead-laced-water-in-flint-a-step-by-step-look-at-the-makings-of-a-crisis (accessed June 7, 2017).

[33] "Lead Poisoning and Health," *World Health Organization*, September 2016, www.who.int/mediacentre/factsheets/fs379/en/ (accessed June 7, 2017).

The social, political, and economic dimensions of the North Carolina and Flint crises are reminders of how pervasive water is in our lives, but the religious links to these public water crises are often less evident. We return to Ezekiel's image to seek out these links.

Water. Flowing out from the threshold of the temple. What if Christian communities' baptismal waters today are Ezekiel's river—a metaphorical and literal fluid faith flowing both to and from a hurting world? What if that river in both symbolic and embodied ways is all of us as Jesus' disciples—flowing out from our churches to make real Ezekiel's promise: Everything will live where the river flows.

Of course, this call extends beyond water. One way we live out or embody what we deem worship's essentials is to link them to the essentials of everyday life. Baptism, the Lord's Supper, Love feasts, the fire of our liturgical candles, the oil of our anointing and healing practices—all of the ordinary-extraordinary stuff of Christian worship arises from and returns to everyday life—to the earth. These worship essentials—these earthy, ordinary elements and actions—they have something to do with our local water basins and watersheds, with local farmers and bakers, with local food-growing practices and food insecurity, and with local economies because local waters, grains, and soils are their sources.

How do we get re-grounded or re-placed in local everyday realities so that we encounter God in all dimensions of our lives whether we are gathered at the font in the Sunday sanctuary or drinking water from our kitchen tap on a Monday? How do we break bread in remembrance of Jesus and recognize Jesus in our midst whether we are passing bread around the Lord's table in church or rolls around the dinner table in a downtown restaurant? How do we drink deeply of the fruit of the vine and experience the mystery of God's redeeming grace flowing through our veins whether we are sharing worship's common cup or sipping wine or grape juice at a meal with friends? How do twenty-first century Christians experience Martin Luther's sixteenth-century wisdom about the Lord's meal—that "God is wholly in the grain and the grain is holy in God"?[34]

These are incarnational questions that have to do with how God indwells all things, how God indwells us. Hinted at in these questions is the power of what some ecological theologians and biblical scholars term "deep incarnational thinking."[35] The God who created mountains and marsupials, dolphins and daffodils—that God takes up residence in our midst.

As theologian Elizabeth Johnson writes, God became flesh—"material, perishable, vulnerable." God became the stuff of everyday life. God, in Jesus, reached "deep into the tissue" of biological and spiritual existence to infuse all bodies—each of us—with God's life and love:[36]

> This "deep" way of reflecting on the incarnation provides an important insight. By becoming flesh the Word of God confers blessing on the whole of earthly reality in its material dimension, and beyond that, on the cosmos in which the Earth exists. Rather than being a barrier that distances us from the divine, this material world becomes a sacrament that can reveal divine presence. In place of spiritual contempt for the world, we ally ourselves with the living God by loving the whole natural world, part of the flesh that the Word became.[37]

[34] Martin Luther as quoted in Larry Rasmussen, "Returning to Our Senses: The Theology of the Cross as a Theology for Eco-Justice," in *After Nature's Revolt: Eco-Justice and Theology,* ed. Dieter Hessel (Minneapolis: Augsburg Fortress Press, 1992), 40–56.

[35] Norman Habel and Cath James, "A Theology of Deep Incarnation and Reconciliation," *Season of Creation* (Norman Habel and the Justice and International Mission Unit, Commission for Mission of the Uniting Church in Australia, Synod of Victoria and Tasmania), http://seasonofcreation.com/wp-content/uploads/2010/04/a-theology-of-deep-incarnation-and-reconciliation.pdf (accessed October 21, 2016). See also Niels Gregerson, "The Cross of Christ in an Evolutionary World," *Dialog: A Journal of Theology* 40: 192–207.

[36] Elizabeth Johnson, "For God So Loved the Cosmos," *US Catholic* 75, no. 4: 18–21.

[37] Ibid.

What, then, are some concrete ways in our everyday lives we can "ally ourselves with the living God" by loving and attending to God's presence in our rivers, streams, and creeks today?

One way is to enliven and embody the fullness of the meaning of one of our words for worship, "liturgy." The word "liturgy" comes from the Greek term *leitourgia*. In Greek city-states of 2,500 years ago where the word originates, liturgy or *leitourgia* was a civic or public engagement term that meant "work of the people." *Leitourgia* signified the offerings people made in service to the public good—anything from street cleaning to bridge building. Later, Christian communities adopted *leitourgia* to mean worship.

Putting the two meanings together invites us to pay attention to the links between the water in church baptisteries and the water that runs through our neighborhoods and cities. Liturgy is the work of the people to praise God in the Sunday sanctuary; liturgy is also how people in their everyday work join God in God's work to redeem the world. Could it be, then, that everyday acts of human living are in their way liturgy?

Some faith communities in Flint seem to know something about this. Much is at stake politically and ecologically in the Flint water crisis that first captured headlines in 2014. But something is at stake for faith communities too, and churches are responding. A coalition of churches in Flint came together across denominational and theological differences soon after the tragedy was made public to speak what they deem to be Gospel truth into the midst of their city's water crisis.

The coalition also decided to provide actual water in the form of hundreds of thousands of bottles of clean water for people to use until the city's water safety is restored:

> "Father, we know the water saves us," North Central Church of Christ member Robert McDaniel prayed on a recent Sunday. The living water of Jesus Christ washes away sins,

McDaniel declared . . . but people depend on water, too, to quench physical thirst, he said. . . . Twenty-four pack cases of water were stacked high inside the church building and its nearby storage facility. . . . Since this city 65 miles north of Detroit declared a state of emergency in mid-December, the North Central Church has distributed between 150,000 and 200,000 bottles of water.[38]

According to a March 2016 article in *The Christian Chronicle,* North Central Church is only one of many Church of Christ churches collecting and distributing water to Flint residents, and other denominational, interdenominational, and religious groups from Presbyterians to Catholics to Baptists to Unitarian Universalists are involved in similar efforts.

Perhaps in these churches' efforts we glimpse Ezekiel's hope and our calling as faith communities today. In these churches' efforts, we see what becomes possible when the river flows from the temple—across the thresholds of communities of faith—into drought-stricken and despairing cities and lives.

Over the last few years, photographer Sheila Hunter and I have been searching out baptistery paintings in North Carolina churches.[39] Many Christian churches baptize by immersion. Some of these churches feature paintings as a part of their indoor baptisteries. The paintings, usually quite large, hang on the wall just over the baptismal pools where new Christians are immersed.

The landscape paintings are often done by local artists and feature a body of water, usually the Jordan River, though sometimes a local

[38] "Thirsty Souls: Churches Help Victims of Flint Water Crisis," *The Christian Chronicle,* March 2016, http://www.christianchronicle.org/article/thirsty-souls-churches-respond-to-flint-water-crisis (accessed October 21, 2016).
[39] Information about baptistery project and photographs can be found at: https://baptistrypaintings.com/(accessed October 21, 2016).

river, stream, or pond is depicted. The intriguing thing about these paintings is that the river or stream in them is painted in such a way that it appears to flow into the actual water in the baptismal pool. The result is a visual and metaphorical intermingling of the imagined waters such as the Jordan River and the actual local tap or well water that has been used to fill the pool.

This intermingled imagery of waters calls forth Ezekiel 47: "Everything will live where the river goes." A related New Testament image also comes to mind:

> Then the angel showed me the river of the water of life, bright as crystal, flowing from the throne of God and of the Lamb through the middle of the street of the city. On either side of the river is the tree of life with its twelve kinds of fruit, producing its fruit each month; and the leaves of the tree are for the healing of the nations. (Rev 22:1-2)

These two biblical images, along with the pictures of stacks of water bottles in Flint churches and baptistery paintings over indoor baptisteries, offer a powerful depiction of God together with God's people working to rehydrate and redeem cities, agricultural regions, and even divided nations, all through the healing of local waters.

Liturgical theologian Linda Gibler writes that "the Universe is God-drenched. Every being, form and particle of the Universe mediates and responds to God's blessing and has something to teach those who listen."[40] We have an opportunity in our worship to name and celebrate our God-drenched universe in all of its awe-inspiring local saturation and to invite worshipers to greater everyday awareness of God's presence and activity in urban streams and rivers, mountain creeks, and even kitchen taps.

[40] Linda Gibler, *From the Beginning to Baptism: Scientific and Sacred Stories of Water, Oil, and Fire* (Collegeville, MN: Liturgical Press, 2010), vii.

A practical way to embody this opportunity is to name in our prayers over baptismal waters God's presence in actual bodies of water and to lament when and where people and places are at risk because of uncared for waters. Communities can offer these prayers by gathering on the banks of local rivers and streams or by providing in worship local water to name and pour and splash and sprinkle.

Faith communities can also stand in solidarity with places like Flint by incorporating prayers or ritual actions in their worship that draw attention to water injustices and invite commitments to bringing about change. Water contamination problems in Flint became prominent national news on January 5, 2016, when Governor Rick Snyder declared the city to be in a state of emergency. January 5 is the eve of Epiphany in the liturgical calendar.

The lectionary readings for the First Sunday after the Epiphany took on deeper meaning as they were spoken in worship on a day when the news was full of the fears and anger of people in Flint who had been exposed to contaminated water. The Old Testament reading for the day was from Isaiah:

> Thus says the Lord,
> he who created you, O Jacob,
> he who formed you, O Israel:
> Do not fear, for I have redeemed you;
> I have called you by name, you are mine.
> When you pass through the waters, I will be with you;
> and through the rivers, they shall not overwhelm you;
> when you walk through fire you shall not be burned,
> and the flame shall not consume you.
> For I am the Lord your God,
> the Holy One of Israel, your Savior.
> I give Egypt as your ransom,
> Ethiopia and Seba in exchange for you.

> Because you are precious in my sight,
> and honored, and I love you,
> I give people in return for you,
> nations in exchange for your life.
> Do not fear, for I am with you;
> I will bring your offspring from the east,
> and from the west I will gather you;
> I will say to the north, "Give them up,"
> and to the south, "Do not withhold;
> bring my sons from far away
> and my daughters from the end of the earth—
> everyone who is called by my name,
> whom I created for my glory,
> whom I formed and made." (Isa 43:1-7)

The Gospel reading was taken from the Gospel of Luke:

> As the people were filled with expectation, and all were questioning in their hearts concerning John, whether he might be the Messiah, John answered all of them by saying, "I baptize you with water; but one who is more powerful than I is coming; I am not worthy to untie the thong of his sandals. He will baptize you with the Holy Spirit and fire. His winnowing fork is in his hand, to clear his threshing floor and to gather the wheat into his granary; but the chaff he will burn with unquenchable fire."

> Now when all the people were baptized, and when Jesus also had been baptized and was praying, the heaven was opened, and the Holy Spirit descended upon him in bodily form like a dove. And a voice came from heaven, "You are my Son, the Beloved; with you I am well pleased." (Luke 3:15-22)

Lament stood at the threshold of worship on that First Sunday after Epiphany / The Baptism of Our Lord as faith communities moved beyond the edges of Christmas celebrations into the season that reveals and illuminates who Jesus was and is. Lament journeyed to Christian faith communities from the streets of Flint on that January 2016 Sunday and implored worshipers to stand with her and in solidarity with the frightened and despairing people of Flint. I crafted this spoken lament for worship on that Sunday:

And she brought forth her first-born child,
womb waters splashing
hopes and tear-drenched dreams
infant life
baptized—
too soon estranged.

Spirit-sparked rivers unleashed
to dance and delight
now tainted
carrying
not-life
alien
uncertainties
"irreversible neurotoxins"
eroding pipelines
and trust
and tender souls.

We weep.
We wait.
We wail.
We wait.
God,
be with us.

Thirsty,
we wait.

We weep.
God, send again—through us—your waters.

The call of Ezekiel's ancient text echoes across centuries and geographies to communities today. The flow of the river cannot stop with our baptisteries but must flow out across the threshold of our churches and into the places where we live. When we say "yes" to this call then Ezekiel's and Revelation's images of crystal-clear, life-giving waters become possibilities.

So, too, does that striking image in Ezekiel of people standing on the riverbanks fishing. That is what the divine guide shows Ezekiel: people from Engedi to Eneglaim to Flint, to right down the road from our own churches and neighborhoods, telling tales of the big one hauled in from dried-out desert gullies turned fish-fertile, fresh-water rivers.

In that image, we glimpse our calling to live worship's essentials. With God, Ezekiel's divine guide announces in this peculiar prophetic book, all things are possible, even the reconstitution of dry bones, rattling, clattering up out of the dust of drought and despair to pull in fish of every kind from God's great river of justice and grace.

Everything lives where the river flows. And we, the community of faith, are in these days, God's river.

Interlude

Seeing Christ in the Abyss[1]

Jesus was made known to them in the breaking of the bread.

—Luke 24:35

What about their lives compels them to take the risk? Whatever it is, they do it. They climb onto unseaworthy vessels and head out into rough waters. Perhaps the persecution or poverty on their home shores makes the perils of rickety, overburdened boats seem small by comparison. Seeking sanctuary, they go.

The realities of migrating people today are harsh and deadly, and I have found myself thinking that Christ must have been asleep in the vessels that capsized in the Mediterranean in recent weeks and months: he seems not to have awakened to rebuke the wind and sea.

But another courageous voice spoke out in May 2016. German Cardinal Ranier Maria Woelki broke Eucharistic bread from a refugee boat altar as he celebrated the Corpus Christi Mass.

The Washington Post featured these words from Woelki in an essay about his celebration of the Mass: "Someone who lets people drown in the Mediterranean also drowns God."[2] I don't think Woelki was referring to the Christ of the Abyss, the famous

---

[1] This reflection first appeared as a blog post for *Unfundamentalist Christians*. Jill Crainshaw, "Seeing Christ in the Abyss," July 13, 2016, www.patheos.com/blogs/unfundamentalistchristians/2016/07/seeing-christ-in-the-abyss/ (accessed June 9, 2017).

[2] Rick Noak, "The Stunning Way a Catholic Cardinal Marked the Death of Refugees in the Mediterranean," *The Washington Post*, May 26, 2016,

statue of Jesus that was placed in the Mediterranean Sea in the 1950s, though the connection is striking. Between January and May 2016, more than 1,400 migrants died in that same sea where the sculpted Jesus, arms lifted up from the deep, offers a watery benediction. Though Woelki did not refer to the statue, he nevertheless sought through his unconventional Eucharistic blessing at that boat-altar to lament refugee drownings in those same waters and call for Christian actions of care.

Migration and immigration realities across the globe are a tangle of issues and as has been the case numerous times throughout history, water has played a part in those issues. The current numbers are staggering. The International Organization for Migration estimates that in 2015 more than one million migrants arrived by sea at European shores. The rhetoric surrounding the surge of asylum requests is often searing and razor sharp. Lives are at stake in the debates. The question arises. How should people of faith respond to the horrors and complexities of migration?

Perhaps our own experiences of being a stranger summon us to care for and welcome the stranger in our midst. After all, we are all in some way migrants. Or our ancestors were. Here in the United States, branches of all of our family trees are heavy with stories of kin who migrated for a wide array of reasons. These ancestral migrants fled or were forced to the United States from Scotland, Ireland, Africa, Germany, Korea, Japan, Afghanistan, India, and other distant shores.

Biblical writers would not be surprised by ancestral or contemporary stories of moving from place to place. Don't settle

---

https://www.washingtonpost.com/news/worldviews/wp/2016/05/26/the -stunning-way-a-catholic-priest-marked-the-deaths-of-refugees-in-the -mediterranean/ (accessed October 21, 2016).

in too much, biblical writers seem to say. We are to be restless, always in search of justice and peace.

Consider Genesis 1:"In the beginning the spirit of God moved over the face of chaos."[3] To move, says Joan Maruskin of Church World Service, is to migrate. God's spirit "migrated" over the face of chaos. From there, throughout Scripture, humankind's story is a migration story. Joseph is sold into slavery but becomes a powerful leader in a foreign land. The Israelites flee Egypt, wander in the wilderness, then migrate into the land of Canaan. People of other cultures already lived there; the Israelites were outsiders and immigrants *to the Promised Land.* Famine chases Naomi across the border into Moab. Jesus and his parents become refugees for a time, crossing the border into Egypt to escape Herod's violence. The disciples leave their homes to follow Jesus; they become itinerant preachers, migrating back and forth across familiar and unfamiliar lands.

This overarching biblical theme of migration enlivens our the-ologies. As people of faith, we join biblical ancestors in seeking that promised land where there is no weeping or pain. Mean-while—until we arrive in that sought-after place—God calls us to do what we can to create God's home here on earth, in our cities and towns. God calls us to create sanctuaries—places of safety and flourishing—for all people.

Again, how are people of faith *as people of faith* to respond to the complexities and horrors of immigration and migration? Not all Christians will agree on legislation or even denominational actions. But perhaps we can embrace our shared strangeness in

[3] Joan M. Maruskin, "The Bible as the Ultimate Immigration Handbook: Written by, for, and about migrants, immigrants, refugees, and asylum seek-ers," prepared for the Church World Service Immigration and Refugee Program, 2003.

this world and then out of that respond with courage to refugees' cries for peace and safety.

Cardinal Woelki's refugee boat-altar stands as a reminder. So does the generous welcome many churches are extending to refugees. God calls us—friends and strangers—to be radically hospitable and restlessly to seek God's justice for all whose migration stories have left them isolated, sometimes drowning, and always seeking renewed life on other shores. Indeed, God calls people of faith to break bread with those who are strangers to us. Remember Luke 24? The resurrected Jesus was right there with the disciples on the road, but they did not recognize him. They asked: Are you the only stranger in Jerusalem who doesn't know what's going on? But then they recognized him in the breaking of the bread.

To break bread with a stranger was—and is—to encounter Jesus. Perhaps when we decide to risk standing in uncertain boats to break bread with and on behalf of wounded strangers and refugees, we embody a Christ who rises up from the watery abyss to calm the raging storm and restore justice, hope, and faith.

Chapter 5

Bearing Witness, Birthing Hope

God, or the gods, are invisible, quite
understandable. But holiness is visible, entirely.

— Mary Oliver[1]

After nine months of anxious waiting, he was here. Tiny hands.
Thick, silky-soft nest of hair. He was here. Marco.

She had not counted on meeting him this early in his vocational
journey. After all, she was not his mother or grandmother. She was
not a doctor or pastor or chaplain. She was just his mother's tutor. A
tutor become friend, and now, out of the blue, she had become a doula
of sorts. She was not an official doula, of course. Today's doulas are
trained ritual artisans who support and accompany mothers through
their pregnancies and birthing processes.[2] Ramona requested Gayle's

---

[1] Mary Oliver, *Felicity* (New York: Penguin Press, 2016), 17.

[2] Louise Eve Ballen and Ann J. Fulcher, "Nurses and Doulas: Complementary
Roles to Provide Optimal Maternity Care," *Journal of Obstetrics, Gynecologic and
Neonatal Nursing* 35 (2006): 304–11. Throughout history, women have supported
each other during births. Some women today seek the presence of a doula to
provide this support. The primary aim of the doula is "to ensure that the woman
feels safe and confident" as she moves through the process of childbirth. See
also Robbie E. Davis-Floyd, *Birth as an American Rite of Passage* (Berkeley:
University of California Press, 2003).

presence for Marco's birth. Gayle showed up. She became Ramona's birthing companion.

"Why am I here in a labor room, coaching a birthing mother?" Gayle texted her friends throughout the long night and morning of Marco's birth. "No one told me teaching multiplication tables to a 7-year-old once a week would add up to this eleven years later."

But Gayle had listened into the depths of the life of her student as she coached her through hours of mathematics homework. Their time together had been about much more than math problems, Gayle knew. Marco's birth story was scripted onto the pages of an uncertain life saga. Even up until the week Marco was born, for all practical purposes, Ramona was homeless. No job. No money. No place to lay her baby's head.

Just one day before Marco's birthing day, Ramona, with Gayle's support, found a dwelling place, a transitional housing program for mothers who are homeless. She moved into her new space on a Friday afternoon. That night she went into labor. When the phone call came, Gayle headed to the hospital; tutoring of another kind was about to begin.

Twenty hours later, all of life—the hopes, fears, joys of the whole world it seemed—rushed together into one powerful moment of effort to push fragile new hopes into the light of day and Gayle was there. A tutor become friend become birthing coach become witness to a word made flesh. Marco, just moments before a womb-held hope, was now a birthed human life held in his mother's arms.

Several Sundays after Marco's birth, I worshiped at my church on the Seventh Sunday of Easter, called Ascension Sunday in my community. Marco was on my mind.

The Scripture reading for that Ascension Sunday was from Acts 1: "Jesus was lifted up, and a cloud took him from their sight" (v. 9). The preacher reminded worshipers: "The end of the Easter season's seven weeks marks Jesus' disappearance from his followers yet again. Jesus' friends had grieved his absence after he died. They celebrated with startled eyes and uncertain hearts the surprise of his resurrection. Now, they will have to grieve again."

"Next Sunday," the preacher said, "is Pentecost. Next Sunday we will remember how Holy Spirit winds blew into the world, stirring up those first followers' courage and urging them to continue Jesus' earthly, everyday work despite his physical absence.

"But on that day when Jesus disappeared into the clouds, his followers didn't know with any certainty that Spirit winds were headed their way a week later. All they knew for sure was that Jesus was gone again."

The preacher's words and the worship service's Ascension Sunday images were familiar to me. I had journeyed through many Easter to Pentecost seasons with this congregation. But Ascension celebrations had never before struck me like that Sunday's celebration did. On this particular Ascension Sunday, I worshiped with a seven-weeks-new human person named Marco on my mind and in my heart. Because of what I knew about Gayle's, Ramona's, and Marco's experiences, my Ascension Sunday worship was seasoned by poignant and concrete longings for certainty about God's presence and activity in human lives.

As Gayle recounted her experience in that labor room, complex theological questions emerged for me. What are we to do with those times in our lives between Ascension and Pentecost when physical assurances of hope are gone and the future is at best unclear and at worst terrifying? What are we to do or say when most of our days or the days of someone we care about are like that uncertain time when Jesus has disappeared and the Spirit had not yet arrived? What do our liturgical practices have to do with actual human experiences like Ramona's?

Marco is here. A beautiful, fragile being birthed onto this life-giving, life-denying, awe-inspiring, terror-inducing earth. What is Marco's future going to be like?

The Gospel reading for a few Sundays before had said something about Jesus' promise that he would not leave his followers orphaned.[3] The psalm for that Seventh Sunday of Easter, Ascension Sunday, spoke of orphans too: "Father of orphans and protector of widows is God in God's holy habitation. God gives the desolate a home to live in" (Ps 68:5-6).

More than ever before, I wanted the promises of those Easter season texts and of the Feast of the Ascension liturgy that day to matter in a concrete way, to sink down roots and bear fruit in the ground of Marco's life. Because Gayle had shared with me Marco's birth story, my ears were tuned now to the sound of an infant's cry, and I wanted the prayer of the day to be less ethereal than it often sounded:

> O God of earth and sky,
> as Jesus came among us in Bethlehem to raise us up
>   to heaven,
> so today we recall his departing from us at Jerusalem to be
>   in all places.
> Though he is hidden from our sight,
> enable us to abide in him
> by the power and grace of the Holy Spirit,
> until his mercy and grace fill your whole creation. Amen.[4]

---

[3] See John 14:18-19: "I will not leave you orphaned; I am coming to you. In a little while the world will no longer see me, but you will see me; because I live, you also will live" (NRSV). This text appears as the gospel reading for the Sixth Week of Easter in Year A in the Revised Common Lectionary.

[4] "Prayers for Ascension Day (or Ascension Sunday)" (Order of St. Luke Press, 2000), http://www.umcdiscipleship.org/resources/prayers-for-ascension-day-or -ascension-sunday (accessed October 26, 2015).

The prayer stirred for me a question: How do those who have no homes abide in God?

As I did on that Sunday, theologians wrestle with the questions that linger in those days between Ascension and Pentecost. What *are* Christian people to make of the absence of the Presence between Ascension and Pentecost or at any time across the span of our individual and communal lives?[5]

The twentieth-century theologian Karl Barth called the days between the two liturgical moments of Ascension and Pentecost a "significant pause" between God's mighty acts.[6] The book of Acts paints an image of this pause. For those first followers of Jesus, as the sun rises on that forty-first day after Easter, Jesus has ascended—gone away—into the clouds. Pentecostal fires have not yet burned away the shrouding mist. Jesus' absence must have been palpable. What were those early disciples—what are we as individuals and communities today who daily

---

[5] I am grateful for a sermon by Ken Carter, whose insights about Karl Barth's "significant pause" and the "in-between" times of faith illustrated by Ascension Sunday, inspired my thinking and research for this chapter. See Carter, "Waiting": A sermon taken from Acts 1:1-11 and preached on Ascension Sunday, May 16, 2010, at Providence United Methodist Church in Charlotte, North Carolina (unpublished sermon).

[6] See Karl Barth, *Credo* (New York: Charles Scribner's Sons, 1962). The phrase Barth uses to describe the ten days between Ascension Day and Pentecost Day—"significant pause"—has been cited often by theologians and preachers. For example, see William H. Willimon, *Interpretation, A Biblical Commentary on Acts* (Atlanta: John Knox Press, 1988); Patricia Datchuck Sanchez, *The Word We Celebrate: Commentary on the Sunday Lectionary, Years A, B, and C* (Lanham, MD: Rowman and Littlefield Publishers, 1989), 43; and Veli-Matti Karkkainen, *Christ and Reconciliation: A Constructive Christian Theology for the Christian World,* vol. 1 (Grand Rapids, MI: Eerdmans, 2013), 360–61. Karkkainen suggests that "ascension" is central to Barth's Christology and quotes Barth's *Church Dogmatics* on the topic: "The most important verse in the ascension story is the one which runs: 'A cloud received him out of their sight' (Acts 1:9). In biblical language the cloud does not signify merely the hiddenness of God, but His hidden presence, and the coming revelation which penetrates this hiddenness." See Karl Barth, *Church Dogmatics*, vol. 3, part 2 (Edinburgh: T. & T. Clark, 1936), 454.

face life-denying challenges, life's aching needs—to do during this ambiguous pause when it settles down into our hearts, minds, and bodies?

Both faith communities and pastors relish those joyous and often
liturgically colorful and jubilant moments when worship and ministry mark and embody God's mighty acts. Energies and spirits tend
to soar as communities move through Advent toward Christmas.
Easter morning's dawn is for many a time of recommitment to Gospel
promises of hope and life again in the midst of despair and death.
Liturgists delight in the textures, sounds, and smells of the Christian
year's most significant moments. God's presence at least seems more
possible during those times. Our visions of who God is and who we
are as God's people are clearer when we are peering into the manger
at Christmas or the empty tomb at Easter.

But the pauses come too, those times when our liturgies are less
trumpeting, when our feet are poised, even restless, for the next steps
away from the empty tomb, but when we have not yet stirred the dust
on whatever roads God wants us to travel into the future. We even
arrive at those times when we are not convinced that we ever saw
Jesus alive in our world at all. Here and there, now and then, we come
in our lives to that span of days between Ascension and Pentecost.
Liturgically, we come to it once each year. We pause, and it is theologi-
cally, liturgically, and practically a significant pause as we anticipate
whatever the season's birthing commences in our lives.

One of the church's tasks during the Ascension to Pentecost pause,
said Barth, is to wait and to pray, "Come, Holy Spirit." [7] Barth may
be right. His advice does after all reflect the Scripture readings for
the day: "While staying with them, Jesus ordered them not to leave
Jerusalem but to wait there for the promise of the Father" (Acts 1:4).

Yes, perhaps we are to wait and pray until the Spirit comes and we
"have been clothed with power from on high" (Luke 24:49, the Gospel

---

[7] See Karl Barth, "Come, Creator Spirit," in *Come, Holy Spirit: Sermons* (Round
Table Press, 1933).

reading for the Feast of Ascension). But what if the wisdom of Gospel faith is also in recognizing this: ministry happens when we wait and pray over seemingly mundane multiplication tables even as we anticipate heart-stopping moments of revelation and transformation. Perhaps the times in between ministry's mighty acts should come with a warning: "Caution! Multiplication tables can and do sometimes lead to labor rooms."

This is, after all, the point of ministry, isn't it? We are called to bear witness. To see. To feel the weight of what we see. To respond to what we see. Yes, we are called to bear witness, and that means being present, if we dare. But being present where? At weddings, funerals, and baptisms, if we are pastoral leaders. At podiums in classrooms, study desks in offices, and pulpits in sanctuaries if we are teachers, preachers, and scholars. But we are also called—all believers, as priests in the priesthood of all believers, are called—to bear witness in those moments when wisdom's wisest and most profound gift is what happens when a young woman and an older woman become for each other promises of hope and new life.

That was the gift Ramona gave to Gayle and Gayle gave to Ramona. They bore witness to each other's lives and saw in each other trustworthiness, hope, care, and love. They became family to each other.

We are called to witness. We are also called to *bear witness.* We are called to be present to profound and powerful Gospel realities that persist during the pauses. We are called to be doulas for those in our communities who long for companions for life's difficult birthing rituals. We are called to be midwives for Gospel realities being birthed in our midst that are not often narrated in sermons or litanies, in speeches or doctrinal analyses. We are called to draw out new meanings of resurrection in each other as Ramona did for Gayle by trusting her to journey with her through the birthing process.

What do liturgical practices or theological, biblical, or liturgical study have to do with this call? One dimension of the connection is exemplified in what I hope theological education accomplishes in the lives of my ministry students. Students invest six semesters of their lives—eighty-one credit hours—in our school's master of divinity program. I hope that after their three years of intensive theological study, my students have more theological knowledge than they did when their anxious palms sweated before that first semester's church history exam.

I also hope that when my students graduate, they are nimbler biblical interpreters and are more aware of biblical intricacies. Though not an Ascension Day text, the Bible's "midwifery" text in Exodus 1 comes to mind for me as I consider how Gayle's, Ramona's and Marco's stories might shape our perspectives on biblical stories and texts:

> The king of Egypt said to the Hebrew midwives, one of whom was named Shiphrah and the other Puah, "When you act as midwives to the Hebrew women, and see them on the birthstool, if it is a boy, kill him; but if it is a girl, she shall live." *But the midwives feared God; they did not do as the king of Egypt commanded them, but they let the boys live.* (Exod 1:15-18 [NRSV])

Perhaps after studying the Bible and homiletics, some of my students, as pastoral leaders, will now pause when they come to familiar texts like Exodus 1. Then, in the pause, instead of their eyes alighting on the usual sermonic cues, they will see in this ancient text, perhaps as if for the first time, Jochebed, Shiphrah and Puah.

Jochebed, Shiphrah, and Puah. Who were they? Jochebed was Moses' mother, while Shiphrah and Puah were midwives before Moses was born. Egypt's Pharaoh commanded them to kill all of the male Hebrew children whose births they witnessed.

But Shiphrah and Puah followed their own callings and delivered the one who delivered Israel. They stood by Jochebed, Moses' mother. They bore witness to Moses' birth. And by doing that they joined Jochebed in birthing liberation, in birthing a people, in birthing a new history of God with God's people.

Biblical scholar David Lose says this about Shiphrah and Puah to those crafting sermons on Exodus 1:

> Two women [Shiphrah and Puah] once made a decision, took
> a chance, and changed the world. It was simultaneously a
> small gesture and heroic act. They disobeyed. And because
> of their act of disobedience God was able to rescue Israel
> from oppression. Their names are Shiphrah and Puah, and
> while you may know them, I'm betting almost no one in your
> congregation does. Which is a shame, because they have
> something to teach us all. [8]

Perhaps my students will pause when they come to Exodus 1 to look and listen for Jochebed, Shiphrah, and Puah.

And perhaps they will hear in the story of Jochebed, Shiphrah, and Puah what other midwives and doulas and birthing mothers across the years have heard God saying to them. Perhaps my students will hear a call to be unexpected and even subversive midwives to world-transforming births. And perhaps because my students see and hear Jochebed, Shiphrah, and Puah through the twenty-first century liturgies they create and the sermons they preach, they will invite people like Gayle and Ramona to hear in these ancient women's stories their own stories. Perhaps they will invite all in their congregations to see and hear God's Story in the stories of all those who are lost or forgotten or diminished by this harsh world.

What I hope for my students and for all worshiping communities is that through their communities' liturgies they, like Jochebed, Shiphrah, and Puah, will become aware of—that they will feel in the life-giving marrow of their bones—those moments of human living when compassion and intelligence, theological acuity and moral

---

[8] David Lose, "The Butterfly Effect," *Dear Working Preacher*, Sunday, August 14, 2011, http://www.workingpreacher.org/craft.aspx?post=1599 (accessed October 16, 2015).

responsibility, theory and practice fuse within them so that their very bodies annunciate God's grace made flesh. That, it seems, is what connects churchly liturgical practices to everyday human realities—our capacity to allow Gospel liturgy (the work of the people) in hospitals and corporate boardrooms, at the city gates and in urban streets to birth Gospel liturgy (the work of the people) in church and vice versa. And more often than not, those annunciating, birthing, midwifing moments grace us in the pauses between the life and ministry events we and others typically highlight as significant. Those midwifing and birthing moments grace us when God seems most absent.

So, what if Barth's "significant pauses" between each season's Ascension and Pentecost moments are expectant pauses? What might that mean, and how can we tap into that meaning and possibility in our worship? How can worshipers like Gayle find in the Sunday worship that happens between the feast days life-giving resonance with their everyday lives? How can Gayle connect liturgy on the Seventh Sunday of Easter—Ascension Sunday—with the birthing ritual she found herself immersed in?

Some comedians are experts in the use of what they term the "pregnant pause." In their performances, they place a beat—a pause— at just the right moment for just the right number of seconds to give the audience time to get the joke. Comedic pauses leave room for listeners to discern subtexts or to catch unspoken nuances. Sometimes a comedian's timing and delivery of a pause are so good the pause becomes a source of humor that extends beyond the original joke. The pause is integral to the joke. Laughter is birthed there. So is depth of meaning.

Theological and liturgical pauses are something like that. Gospel narrative pauses are too. Consider all that is unspoken but felt just beneath the surface during those days after Jesus' death before his resurrection. And what about after the resurrection when Jesus was somehow with the disciples again? Can we imagine the wonder-sparked laughter that might have erupted at that dinner table when Jesus' friends realized that the man they had been talking to as a stranger on Luke's road to Emmaus was Jesus? Can we feel the awe-inspired hilarity that must have escaped their hearts, minds, and bodies once the disciples grasped that Jesus was indeed alive again?

Those comedic, pregnant pauses can be powerful and prophetic. They make space for us to bear witness to Gospel truths that are at the same time beyond-the-pale outlandish and too good to be true. They make space for something liberating and redeeming beyond our wildest imaginings to be born into our midst, despite all evidence to the contrary and even out of the depths of our despair.

That is perhaps why Sunday worship itself can sometimes be considered liminal time—boundary or threshold time. Each Sunday's worship—even worship on those most event-full Sundays like Easter Sunday—is, in a sense, a pregnant pause.

Or it can be. That is one of the contemporary challenges and opportunities of worship. Our liturgies can invite worshipers to set aside preconceived notions and unhealthy assumptions and plunge into life's deepest and rawest realities.

Ritual theorist Victor Turner put it this way in the 1960s: Liminal people—perhaps liturgical people?—are "neither here nor there; they are betwixt and between the positions assigned and arrayed by law, custom, convention, and ceremony."[9] That is what makes transformation possible. Liminal people shed those things that separate them from others. They open themselves to fresh possibilities. They open themselves to what Turner terms "communitas," a heightened sense of connectedness that happens when people come together and share as equals about their lives.[10]

---

[9] Victor Turner, *The Ritual Process: Structure and Anti-structure* (Berlin: Walter de Gruyter, 1969), 95.

[10] Ibid., 94–130.

When worship becomes liminal space, worshipers pause and for a moment shed the costumes—the social signs and stigmas, the symbols of hierarchy and power—with which we so easily become garbed as we move through educational systems, as we are socialized as citizens in particular places, and as we take our places in societal racial, ethnic, political, and economic hierarchies. That is one of worship's greatest possibilities. When we enter into the unstable liminal spaces of worship, we have the chance, all of us together as equals, to birth in our midst the body of Christ.

One challenge to the concept of liturgical liminality is to its assumed temporal quality. Worshipers enter into worship's liminal space but then return to their everyday work and lives and whatever stability or instability characterizes those lives. Worship may announce hope and worshipers may cling with whole-hearted belief to that hope, but Monday brings with it a return to life's inequalities and injustices. Even so, liturgies over time promise us that the overall arc of the Christian story emphasizes the temporariness of human life and this world. We can celebrate liminality in worship because we have the promise of God's future reign. We can live betwixt and between because the Gospel story promises that Jesus will return. The absence of the Presence is not forever.

Even as we celebrate the possibilities of God's future reign, however, the story of Jochebed, Shiprah, and Puah along with Ramona's and Gayle's stories are a reminder. Some people in our communities live in a perpetual state of betwixt and between, of not belonging anywhere, of having no place to dwell. Marco and Ramona did not need a liminal pause. What they needed in their here and now was stability. Food. Shelter. Clothing. A steady source of income. These things are necessary if any of us are to survive, if any of us are to move toward the flourishing promised us as God's beloved children.

How does or can liturgy and liturgy's liminal spaces lead to justice—to a foretaste of God's reign *now*—for those who live on life's margins?

The purpose of liturgy, says liturgical theologian Aidan Kavanagh, is to "undercut and overthrow" life's unjust and unstable structures so that worshipers can stand for a moment—can pause perhaps?—in the cracks of reality and experience the God of radical justice.[11] When liturgy accomplishes this purpose, then liturgy becomes a space where worshipers encounter in the marrow of their bones what is most fully human and are urged to imagine how and where to glimpse this same fullness of humanity—God's presence in Christ—in the midst of everyday life and living. Liturgy promises God's future reign, but it also insists that we can bear in our bodies and souls now—we can bear witness now—those promises as we embody God's radical hospitality, justice, and grace in our everyday "between Ascension and Pentecost" lives.

Liturgical scholar Nathan Mitchell describes such a liturgical experience this way:

> The drama of the liturgy is nothing more or nothing less than the drama of human history, permeated by God's presence. . . . Christian worship is inherently worldly. Its primary symbols are drawn from the messiest activities of human life: giving birth and dying, washing and smearing bodies with oil, eating and drinking, unburdening one's heart in the presence of another. All of this is the septic stuff of the world's drama and the stuff of Christian liturgy as well.[12]

If Mitchell is right, then perhaps Ramona's and Gayle's experiences in the hospital labor and delivery rooms were themselves liturgy. God was there, in that messy and glorious moment of birth. Ramona experienced it. Gayle witnessed it. Now Gayle can seek it in her

---

[11] Aidan Kavanagh, *The Elements of Rite: A Handbook of Liturgical Style* (Collegeville, MN: Liturgical Press, 1990), 40.

[12] Nathan Mitchell, "The Spirituality of Christian Worship," *Spirituality Today* 34, no. 1 (March 1982): 10.

church's worship, in that "significant pause" between Ascension and Pentecost that draws our attention to the absence of the Presence. She can seek the wonders of Marco's birth waters in the baptismal waters of her church's font. She can seek the nourishing promises of a mother's milk measured out just so at her liturgy's feast table.

In that Resurrection Day labor room, the boundary markers between church and the world, between the sacred and secular, disappeared, and Gayle found herself bearing witness as a young woman birthed hope. And for a moment—for a significant pause—a crack appeared in the order of things, and Gayle glimpsed in Ramona's face, in the face of that newborn, and in the faces of doctors and nurses—perhaps even in her own face looking back at her in the hospital bathroom mirror—the face of God. And that is liturgy of the most poignant and radical and prophetic kind.

Bearing witness—pause—birthing hope. Life's pauses are sources of uncertainty but they are also sources of grace. How many people in our world today struggle to live somewhere between Ascension and Pentecost? To some degree that is where each of us lives every day throughout our lifetimes. We wrestle with what it means to be human even as we seek what it means to incarnate the mysteries of God's Spirit. God calls God's people to face life's betwixt and between spaces and bear witness. Our liturgies should call us too—to taste and see birth and death in all of their unfettered force and in all of their remarkable simplicity. To listen. Linger. Wonder. Laugh. Stand with.

For when we undertake these things, sometimes, whether during ministry's mighty moments or in the pauses between, sometimes when we bear witness, the world and its people, by the grace of God, birth hope. And that, of all things, can be none other than liturgy.

Marco is here. [Pause.] "Can I get a witness?"

Interlude

Bearing Witness and Baking Bread

Research for a class on sacraments and ordinances—the Lord's Supper and baptism—took me to local artisan bread bakeries. I wanted to learn from expert bakers about how they birth both the delicious breads we enjoy at daily meal tables and the bread we break at the Lord's table. I wanted to know about the bread-birthing wisdom that resides in their heads, hearts, and hands.

Gus is the baker at one of my favorite local bakeries. He welcomed me into the bakery's kitchen and shared with me the process of turning flour, water, and yeast into that crusty sourdough bread I love to crunch my teeth into at lunch or dinner. Though a young man, Gus has been baking bread for many years. He learned much of what he knows by doing what he does—mixing, kneading, shaping, waiting, and baking—day after day, six days a week.

When I asked Gus what advice he would give to beginning bakers, his answer was something like this: "Don't be afraid to try something new."

Ever since Gus offered this advice and shared the importance of using fresh, local ingredients for making bread, I have thought I could taste a kind of fearlessness and mystery in Gus's breads. Gus bakes sweet and savory breads from whole wheat, rye, and white flours. Gus also mixes into his dough fresh herbs and spices and other flavors that delight the nose and intensify the taste of his breads. The fearlessness and mystery I now taste along with these delectable gifts come, I think, both from Gus's story as a baker and from how connected bread is to earth's life forces.

Many bakers I have known see bread making as a spiritual exercise that connects them to life forces. Gus helped me to see and taste what they mean by this. A key ingredient in the sourdough bread that is Gus's specialty is yeast. Yeast is that mysterious substance that initiates the fermentation process that makes bread dough rise.

But the process does not happen without the help of the bread baker. Bakers harness and cultivate life forces—grains from the earth and the fungus we call yeast—by skillfully mixing and kneading ingredients to develop gluten, the rubbery component of wheat, so that the dough traps the bubbles of gas released by the yeast as it reproduces. Gifts of the earth, taken, mixed, and kneaded by human hands, become the staff of life.

Gus is not the only bread baker who shared with me the wisdom of his hands. Penny did too. Penny is eighty years old. She has baked bread through many life seasons. Like Gus, Penny took me into her home kitchen. Penny's bread-baking wisdom inspired the following sermon based on John 6:1-15.

Bread of Earth, Bread of Life, Bread of Heaven

"Where are we going to buy bread for these people to eat?"

—John 6:5

Bread. It has come a long way since Egyptians first baked flatbread thousands of years ago.[1] Consider all the kinds of bread we can buy today: pumpernickel, rye, chocolate cherry sourdough, and chipotle cheddar. But when we get right down to it, bread is made of basic things: flour, water, salt, and leaven.

---

[1] For a history of bread and baking, see H. E. Jacob, *Six Thousand Years of Bread: Its Holy and Unholy History* (New York: Skyhorse Publishing, 2007).

Bread is the fruit of fertile fields and work of human hands. It is golden-crusted loaves passed from me to you to the stranger. We cannot live without either the bread or the sharing: in both we encounter God's grace.

So we come to the bread story in the Gospel of John. The setting: more than ten thousand weary feet are stirring up the dust of the dirt road as people make their way to where they have heard they can find Jesus. Jesus sees them headed toward him, and his first thought is for their physical well-being; his first concern is hospitality.

Jesus turns to Phillip: "Where are we going to buy bread for these people to eat?"

Phillip answers: "Even if we had six months' wages (and we don't), we couldn't buy enough for this many people."

Phillip's answer is the pragmatic answer. Jesus can't just send someone to the store for a few loaves of white Wonder Bread; a gathering of this size requires advanced planning and loaves baked ahead of time. Phillip sees the mathematical and economic problem: "We have no money. These people have no money." [2]

In Tiberias where the crowd is gathering, bread is power. These sharecroppers and tenant farmers, beggars and day laborers making their way to Jesus can't afford to buy bread. Jesus' disciples can't afford to buy bread. So, where indeed are they going to get food for these people to eat?

"This boy has five barley loaves and two fish."

Andrew is optimistic—for a moment. But then the reality sets in.

"But what is that with all these people?"

---

[2] Alyce M. McKenzie, "Mind the Gap: The Feeding of the 5000," http://www.patheos.com/ Progressive-Christian/Mind-the-Gap-Alyce-McKenzie -07-20-2012.html (accessed October 21, 2016).

Jesus takes the boy's bread and gives thanks. Their hungry stomachs stop growling, while there are baskets of bread left over. Simple, everyday actions satisfy an unplanned-for crowd.

But that satisfying meal was offered by Jesus. How can you and I feed *five thousand* people? One in nine people worldwide faces chronic hunger today: people right here in our city go to bed at night not sure if they will have enough food for their children when the sun rises. Yes, we live, you and I, between Andrew's hopeful "here are some biscuits and fish" and his discouraged "but what difference can that make?" We live somewhere between the five loaves and the twelve baskets left over. We long for the disasters of injustice to be rectified but that has not happened yet. Even if we are committed to feeding hungry people or to changing policies or transforming how food is grown and distributed—the needs are overwhelming. How do we keep from losing hope? From growing weary? We need a miracle.

Then Penny's bread starter comes to mind.

Bread starter, flour, water, and yeast: the ingredients sound simple enough. But bread starter demands the baker's attention. Starter has to be fed regularly and bread has to be baked with it regularly. Baking bread with starter requires commitment.

Penny made the commitment. She started baking bread some years ago.

And she kept on baking.

Late at night. Bread rising with the morning sun.

She kept on baking.

Penny says she's been baking bread for three or four years, but I think she's been baking that bread for, oh, for forever. I can't recall a family event when that bread's sustaining goodness wasn't present.

Penny has two bread starters going now. She bakes twelve loaves of bread each week to share with friends, with folks in nursing homes, with neighbors—with people who are hungry in all the ways people can be hungry.

So, let's do some math: twelve loaves per week for four years. That's 2,496 loaves of bread. Penny is well on her way to 5,000 with some left over. And that count doesn't include the loaves baked by the friend who gave Penny the starter or the loaves baked by the people to whom Penny has given starter.

Only one miracle story appears in all four Gospels—the story of Jesus feeding the crowd. God means for hungry people to be fed.

But John's story is unique. That young boy? Only in John. What is the importance of this detail of the child? Remember what happens after the meal:

> When the people saw the sign that he had done, they began to say, "This is indeed the prophet who is to come into the world." When Jesus realized that they were about to come and take him by force to make him king, he withdrew again to the mountain by himself. (John 6:14-15)

After the people's hunger has been satisfied, Jesus slips away out of sight so that the people cannot make him king.

I hear a message in this. John's bread story is no *panem et circenses*. *Panem et circenses*. The Latin means "bread and circuses." On occasion, first-century Roman rulers doled out free bread and cheap circus entertainment to appease poor citizens. The practice was common in many countries. In Rome, it was bread and circuses, in Spain, bread and bullfights, and in Russia, bread and spectacle. People in power used food and games for political gain.[3]

---

[3] Carl D. Roth, "Bread and Circuses or Bread of Life," *Grace Lutheran Church, Missouri Synod*, 2011, http://www.graceelgin.org/worship/transcripts /Bread_and_Circuses_or_Bread_of_Life.html (accessed October 22, 2016).

But what Jesus does with the bread in John is no mere spectacle or political ploy. A child shares what he has, and Jesus honors the gift. Jesus blesses that barley bread and pickled fish—poor people's food. And then? Jesus does not appease the crowd. And he refuses to let them be mere consumers of God's bounty. Jesus empowers each child, woman, and man in the crowd to share what they have.

Perhaps *that* is the miracle. We are fed by the bread of life. Then we decide in the face of all evidence to the contrary, in the face of whatever fears threaten to chase us away, in the face of the horror and tragedy of hunger in our world: God can use me—us—to make a difference in our cities and neighborhoods. God can use me—us—to respond to injustices all around us. God can use me—us—to say "no" to racism, to resist hatred. God can use me—us—to feed five thousand people—one hungry person, one loaf, one conversation, one day, one moment of fearless, persisting commitment at a time. Even if it takes a lifetime.

"Where are we going to buy bread for these people to eat?"

Phillip focuses on the math—"how" can we make this happen. Jesus simply asks "where." The same Jesus who blessed the bread that day, who called himself the bread of life—that same Jesus said in that same Gospel: "I came that you might have life and have it more abundantly." When we embrace that promise in our lives—when we embrace who we are in God's image—well, that is the math of everyday miracles. When we give what we have—Jesus blesses it and there is enough and more—beyond our wildest imaginings.[4]

---

[4] Other sources for this sermon: Gail R. O'Day, "Between Text and Sermon: John 6:1-5," *Interpretation* (2000); Rachel Mann, "The Politics of Breaking Bread (Trinity 8, John 6:1-15)," *Political Theology Today*, July 23, 2012, http://www.politicaltheology.com/blog/politics-breaking-bread-trinity-8-john-61-21/ (accessed October 21, 2016).

Chapter 6

Last Year's Nest

A voice is heard in Ramah, lamentation and bitter weeping.
Rachel is weeping for her children; she refuses to be comforted
for her children, because they are no more.

—Jeremiah 31:15

If Rachel's lament is an act of faithfulness making room for
authentic doxology, Mary's praise is steeped in prophetic faith.
If Rachel's lament and her refusal of consolation await the time
of new praise of God, Mary's praise and exultation are fully
aware of the reality of pain and loss. For Mary, like Rachel, will
lose her child, and the sword of grief will pierce her heart too.

—Kathleen D. Billman and Daniel L. Migliore, *Rachel's Cry* [1]

Come, Lament.
Bring your tears.
Scatter them along rocky trails,
dissipating petals of unrefined truth
to water dry paths.

---

[1] Kathleen D. Billman and Daniel L. Migliore, *Rachel's Cry: Prayer of Lament and Rebirth of Hope* (Eugene, OR: Wipf and Stock Publishers, 1999), 3.

Lean in close, Lament.
Place your wizened head
on weighed down shoulders;
whisper-sing in aching ears.

      —Jill Crainshaw

I rescued an empty nest last spring in the rain. I don't know why I rescued the nest. No one lives in it. It was last year's nest.[2]

I was in my car, pulling out of the driveway to head somewhere (I no longer remember to where) when I saw the nest in the middle of the road in front of my house. Instead of driving by or over it, I stopped the car, stepped out into the springtime deluge, and hurried over to the nest, looking up and down the street for other cars (and for the eyes of curious neighbors) as I went.

The nest was beautiful, perfect in its construction, with a single strand of sapphire yarn woven into its middle. How the nest had gotten dislodged from its place in the tree branches and fallen to the ground without being destroyed, I did not know, but my hair was beginning to drip, so this was not the time for intensive critical reflection. I picked up the nest. I looked up and down the street again, this time because I realized that I had no plan for relocating or repurposing the nest. The nest was fragile and soggy, and I was now rain damp and late for where I was headed. So I laid the nest at the base of a tree in the sidewalk buffer and dashed back to my car.

Sometimes I think I spend far too much time rescuing last year's nests. How do we decide, after all, how much energy to give to preserving last year's architectural delights and how much to use building for this year and the future?

---

[2] I first reflected on this experience in a blog post for *Unfundamentalist Christians*. See Jill Crainshaw, "Last Year's Nest," April 15, 2015, www.patheas.com /blogs/unfundamentalistchristians/2015/04/last-years-nest/ (accessed June 8, 2017).

The question pertains to many things in my life. Because I am a Christian minister and professor of worship, I cannot refrain from linking the image of the nest with the work I do, thinking about, teaching, and embodying Christian worship during these times of uncertainty about the future of so many Christian communities. The intricate magnificence of some of last year's nests speak to twenty-first-century worship challenges. Last year's nests hold precious, life-shaping memories. They nurtured possibilities and provided launching pads for nestlings' first flights.

In many Christian communities, we are discovering again how those first followers of Jesus became community and worshiped together. We are rediscovering and embodying some of the life-giving gifts of those early Christians' nests. Some of these rediscoveries remind us of the Gospel's enduring grace-filled power and are vital for liturgical and communal flourishing today.

But we still have work to do. People today seek new kinds of nests, new approaches to worship music, prayer, baptism and the Lord's Supper, and preaching. We need new approaches and ideas that speak to the unique realities of our peculiar times and places. We need fresh perspectives on theology and biblical stories from communities too often ignored or silenced within Christian history. Last year's nests, as comfortable as they may be for some of us, were not and are not always hospitable places for all of God's people. We need provocative and creative voices to remind us that God's Gospel justice making still eludes us today when we hold on with too much caution and fear to nests that are emptying if not already abandoned.

One reason some Christian communities wrestle with their versions of last year's nests may be related to Christianity's, perhaps even our larger society's, loss of the capacity to lament. I am surprised to have arrived at this conclusion when justice making seems to be our generation's most pressing need. How could Gospel justice seeking and justice making not be front and center during these times when children die of abuse, when refugees fleeing violence drown in the Mediterranean Sea, when mothers in communities of color fear everyday for the lives of their fathers, husbands, daughters, and sons? How could Gospel justice making not be a primary force behind our worship and our proclamation in times and places where God's good creation is being ravaged and food insecurity spirals out of control in some communities? The physical and spiritual well-being of many people—even their very survival—needs our passionate attention to the Gospel's promises of peace and grace and abundant life for all people.

But what if lament and justice are inseparable? And what if we have forgotten or ignored the necessary relationship between pain, protest, and praise?

Reconsidering Lament

The societal and churchly penchant for holding on too tightly to romanticized (and thus to a degree fictionalized) versions of "the way things have always been" has for some time perplexed me. We do injustices to ourselves, each other, and our communal well-being when we resist letting go of interpretations of the Bible and assumptions about social and cultural realities that ignore or do not adequately attend to the concrete inequities and needs of our times.

What do we do when the "consolations of orthodox theology and conventional pastoral care"[3] do nothing to speak to our precarious human existence and the heartrending groans that are sometimes wrenched from that existence?

We lament—if we remember how.

We lament, and as preacher Samuel Proctor says, we do the best we can with the tools and understandings we have at hand to transpose Jesus "from a world of goats, camels, fig trees, and mustard seeds

---

[3] Billman and Migliore, *Rachel's Cry*, 3.

to a world of crack, teenage gun fights, child abuse, stealing in high places, and education without values, keeping alive his transforming and saving power generation after generation."[4] That is one of the Gospel's gifts, Proctor says: "Jesus promised that new truth would be given and that the Comforter would lead us to such new truths."[5] But our ability to discern and name new truths and to decide what to do with lingering truths depends to some degree on our willingness to lament—to lament those realities that are dealing death to people, communities, and the earth, and to lament and then let go of those things we must relinquish in order to create space for new voices, ideas, and insights.

A lament or lamentation is a passionate expression of grief, such as wailing, sobbing, crying, or even protesting. We have not forgotten in our world today how to weep. Mothers and fathers weep for their sons' and daughters' futures when gun violence rumbles through their neighborhoods. Spouses weep with their beloveds when a doctor speaks "cancer" into their lives. We weep when the world and its ever-present pain are "too much with us."[6] Yes, many people in communities across the globe, perhaps many of us, have in our weeping echoed in despair the haunting words of Psalm 22 that Jesus cried out in protest from the cross: "My God, why have you forsaken me?"

As Scott Ellington notes, however, biblical lament holds more than individual pain or tears. Biblical lament "is the experience of loss suffered within the context of relatedness."[7] The kind of heartache that accompanies great loss is deeply personal but the cloud of witnesses,

---

[4] Samuel D. Proctor, *The Certain Sound of the Trumpet: Crafting a Sermon of Authority* (Valley Forge, PA: Judson Press, 1994), 9–10.

[5] Ibid.

[6] William Wordsworth, "The World Is Too Much with Us," Academy of American Poets, poets.org (accessed October 23, 2016).

[7] Scott A. Ellington, *Risking Truth: Reshaping the World through Prayers of Lament* (Eugene, OR: Wipf and Stock, 2008), 7.

both historic and contemporary, that surround those in pain—to listen, hold vigil, weep with—prevents our weeping from being an isolating experience. The communal embrace that accompanies pain characterizes authentic lament. Lament arises from and returns to communities of faith and trust, and because of this communal dimension, lament—even lament's wordless, soundless contortions—is sometimes the only thing that keeps people going when everything good about life seems lost. The very fact of our humanity—its fragility and mortality—needs lament.

Theologians Billman and Migliore go so far as to call lament a "precondition of authentic, honest praise."[8] They tune their ears to Rachel's lament in Jeremiah as their example:

> Thus says the Lord:
> A voice is heard in Ramah,
> lamentation and bitter weeping.
> Rachel is weeping for her children;
> she refuses to be comforted for her children,
> because they are no more. (Jer 31:15)

How can Rachel—any Rachel in any time or place—ever find hope again in the face of the kind of pain that sears our hearts when we lose children? How can the Rachel in the apartment complex down the street continue to live when the blood of her murdered child has soaked into her neighborhood's soil? How can a fleeing Rachel, giving birth to a child on an unseaworthy refugee vessel on a stormy sea, ever again vocalize praise? How can the Rachel who "will work for food" to support his family find the energy to sing of God's grace?

And yet, Rachel's disturbing wails for her children, Billman and Migliore say, keep "open the possibility of once again praising

---

[8] Billman and Migliore, *Rachel's Cry*, 3.

God, not falsely or mechanically, but from the heart."[9] How can this be? Saying that lament is the precondition for praise seems to risk justifying those life happenings that are the cause of lament. Without question caution is in order if we move toward reclaiming lament as central to faith.

But Billman and Migliore argue that lament does the opposite of validating pain and injustices in our world. Genuine lament, they insist, keeps open the possibility of doxology because it refuses to hide the intensity of loss beneath the veneer of an idealized past or a sentimentalized spirituality. And communities that make room for genuine lament let go of explicit and subtle expectations that lament remains muffled until it can be vocalized in melodies of triumphant overcoming.[10]

Lament keeps her foot in the door to comfort us because of her open acknowledgement of and respect for the realities of humanity's raw and life-altering pain. Even people in the most horrific pain, when that pain is acknowledged by others, reach toward their own peculiar soul-felt and life-sustaining belief that God is at the same time both nowhere to be found and still somehow a possibility, even if that possibility exists only in the faces and touches of caring community members.[11] To behold another's pain and to have one's pain beheld and then to dwell in that pain in community is itself a kind of doxology, a kind of praise reinterpreted or reimagined as shared lament.

Come, Lament, and Visit Us in Our Travails

Lament visited when Daniel's uncle was murdered. She was not a welcome visitor, but she showed her face through communal care in a place where hearts were rent.

[9] Ibid.
[10] Ibid., 4.
[11] Ellington, *Risking Truth*, 7.

Daniel's family crossed borderlands from Mexico into the United States before Daniel was born. Daniel was fifteen and living in North Carolina with his family when his uncle was shot outside of a local bar. When Daniel's uncle was murdered, I went to the funeral. Lament was there. She was present in the wails of sisters who held onto one another; Lament *does* dwell in blood-spattered city streets. Lament was there in the Latino men lined up behind the back pews, encircling we mourners like the protective arms of God.

Lament was also there when the priest spoke eucharistic words. The Catholic service was entirely in Spanish, so I stumbled from word to word, but the rhythms were wise with ancient familiarity and powerful with always-new promise. The liturgy that day connected us to one another, as different as we were and are. Lament connected us too as in those liturgical moments fragile and inadequate human words faded into unfathomable depths of holy mystery.

Lament: she was Holy Presence on that day of the funeral. She was Holy Presence for Daniel's family on a day when God and any hope of redemption or healing seemed absent. Lament forged community in familiar and unexpected ways on that day of mourning.

Biblical scholar Walter Brueggemann says that the presence of lament is necessary to "redress the distribution of power" in a world of inequities that lead to injustice and pain:

> One loss that results from the absence of lament is the loss of genuine covenant interaction, since the second party to the covenant (the petitioner) has become voiceless or has a voice that is permitted to speak only praise and doxology. Where lament is absent, covenant comes into being only as a celebration of joy and well-being. Or in political categories, the greater party is surrounded by subjects who are always "yes-men and women" from whom "never is heard a discouraging word." Since such a celebrative, consenting

silence does not square with reality, covenant minus lament
is finally a practice of denial, cover-up, and pretense, which
sanctions social control. [12]

When Lament is allowed to live out loud as an expected and accepted
part of faith, believers have the freedom to voice not only their deep
sorrows but also their outrage and protest toward a God who allows
horrific violence, death, and injustice to persist.

Standing alongside each other in the presence of Lament, believers
can demand an explanation for what life or theology or God has given
them. When faith makes ample room for lamenting protest, it becomes
a faith that brings not only to God but also to public places resolute
refusal to accept systemic injustices of any kind. [13]

This happened for Daniel and his family. Vigils for Healing is
a nonprofit, interfaith ministry in Winston-Salem, North Carolina,
where Daniel lives. The ministry's initial aim when it began in 2006
was "to hold public spiritual observances at every murder site in
Forsyth County, North Carolina." As vigils were held in places throughout the county, the ministry's founders gave voice to the breadth and
depth of their mission:

> Vigils for Healing is an advocacy and educational organiza-
> tion whose two-fold mission is to promote healing for people
> affected by violent death, and to change community reaction
> from passive acceptance to active rejection of violence on
> moral, ethical, and spiritual grounds. We call on the power
> of God and a caring community to promote healing for ev-
> eryone affected by violence, including those arrested for the
> murder and their loved ones who also suffer. We reclaim the

[12] Walter Brueggemann, "The Costly Loss of Lament," *The Psalms: The Life
of Faith*, ed. Patrick D. Miller (Minneapolis: Fortress, 1995), 98–111.
[13] Ibid.

sites of violent death and the surrounding neighborhood as life-affirming space. The vigils provide a forum for people to publicly express their feelings about violence and their empathy for the suffering of neighbors. [14]

Vigils for Healing has invited Lament and her provocative, community-gathering presence into some of the most pain-saturated places in Winston-Salem. Daniel's family agreed to let Vigils for Healing hold a vigil on the street where Daniel's uncle was killed.

Vigils, generally understood, are held to keep watch through the night or to stay alert to guard something. On the day of the watch-keeping for Daniel's uncle, people from all over the city gathered at the spot where gunshots had rung out and a man's blood had seeped into the ground. People gathered to be alert to the reality of the horror that had happened on that piece of ground.

After an opening prayer, a family member spoke tearful words in broken English. Vigil Voices, a choir made up of community volunteers, sang a hymn. Then the liturgist asked the uncle's young son to help her pour water that had been blessed into that bloodthirsty soil. As I stood with the community while the boy poured the water, I felt something unspeakable pour out from and then somehow into my own soul.

The boy who poured the water may have been too young to understand the symbolic meaning of that act, but I suspect and hope that something about the bodily gesture lingers with him and with all of us who were present. I hope that the possibilities that dwell in shared lament somehow got into the marrow of that boy's bones. I hope that act of shared lament births in him a life flow of healing that can sustain him in the years to come. And I hope that when he finds himself

[14] Available at http://www.vigilsforhealing.org/pages/about.html (accessed June 8, 2017).

in circumstances that threaten life, he will remember in his very body that symbolic act of quenching the thirst of life-denying soil in the presence of Lament's soul-keeping community.

Our communities need Lament.

Lament and Sustainability

What does authentic lament look like and sound like today?

Tied to this question are two questions common to our era: What ideas or resources or lifestyles do we want and need to sustain in this age of increasing emphasis on sustainability? And what has to die or what do we have to relinquish in order to sustain those things we want to sustain?

What are we to do with last year's nests?

These questions about sustainability are not often asked when we think about lament. We also don't often think about Christian worship in terms of sustainability. Could this be because we are no longer clear (if we ever were) about the relationship between sustainability, grief, and lament? What can we learn from or create in our liturgical practices to support a renewed, even liberating understanding of this complex triad?

A Google search uncovers in the midst of a sea of bloggers, organizations, and even advertisers who tout sustainability, a handful of writers who are asking, "What is it that we want to sustain?" Implied by the question is what Chris Agnos, a blogger for an Australian community called UPLIFT (Universal Peace and Love in a Field of Transcendence) and founder of Sustainable Humans, explores in his work on sustainability: "It takes life to sustain life." [15]

---

[15] Chris Agnos, "What Is Sustainability?" *UPLIFT,* May 2, 2015, http://uplift connect.com/sustainability/ (accessed October 25, 2016).

Sometimes, Agnos says, we find ourselves seeking to sustain conflicting entities or ideas:

> While jobs may increase our own ability to sustain ourselves in the economy we have constructed, many of these jobs also erode the capacity of the planet to support life. Nearly every product we bring to market takes life to create it. Let's take an iPhone for example. The materials that comprise an iPhone need to be mined from all around the world, which causes the destruction of a local ecosystem. Oil is needed to ship these components all throughout the assembly process and to bring the final product to the local store near you. The phone requires electricity to keep it functional, which also requires the extraction of fuel. Everything we do or create costs something real, and I don't mean money. To create anything, we must take it from somewhere else, and that cost is usually the life of an animal or a tree or a plant. [16]

Again, it takes life to sustain life and lifestyles: sacrifice and sustainability are connected.

Nothing lives without the sacrifice of something else. To live each day, people consume food, water, and other elements that come from the earth. But we are not often aware when we are eating lunch of the deaths of plants or animals required to provide our lunch. We are not attentive very often to the links between consumption and sacrifice.

Market-driven economies perpetuate this lack of awareness. What markets know is that consumers pay attention to the cost of things they want and need to buy. We notice the rise and fall of gas prices during vacation times when we want to travel or when the cost to travel to work outpaces our incomes. We pay attention to how the prices of products like cereal or sneakers vary from one company to

---

[16] Ibid.

another and question what accounts for the difference as we decide which brand to buy. One result? Corporations and advertisers work hard to persuade consumers that their brands or styles are worth whatever they cost.

Corporate America also works to persuade consumers to purchase products and experiences on credit. A popular MasterCard tagline illustrates how creative corporations can be in their advertising efforts: "There are some things money can't buy. For everything else there's MasterCard."

This MasterCard ad campaign is an old nest in the world of marketing. The first "priceless" television commercial ran in 1997. It features purchases of tickets, hot dogs, and sodas a father makes with his credit card at a baseball game. The commercial ends with a shot of father and son together in the stands and the proclamation: "Real conversation with 11-year-old son: priceless." With the "priceless" ad campaign, MasterCard connects the purchase of products with the creation of priceless experiences.

MasterCard has discovered in this long-running ad campaign the power and allure of human communal moments and linked them to the supporting elements of those experiences that can be purchased. Not named in the ad campaign is the link between those supporting elements (the hot dogs, airline travel, production of goods) and the sacrifices of hourly wage human workers and of increasingly "priceless" earth resources.

Theologian Chris Chapple argues for a different way of thinking about consumption and sacrifice as we work to preserve the earth's resources for future generations:

> In order to foster a sustainable economic and political and psychological and spiritual state of affairs, people need to adopt new models of sacrifice. Rather than feeling punished by high costs for goods and services, the new sacrificial order

might help people return to a sense of immediacy and aliveness. As food becomes more expensive, it becomes more cherished. Similarly, travel, whether for work or pleasure, will require careful consideration not only of cost but of its wider impact on the production of carbon. Personal identity, rather than being tied to the acquisition and manipulation of things, can be measured in terms of one's connectivity with others and with the primary source of revelation, the earth community. In conclusion, sacrificial wisdom, though differing from one cultural context to another, holds promise as a conceptual and practical resource to inspire people to take the steps necessary for personal, social, and economic sustainability.[17]

How do these insights from Chapple relate to Christian understandings of lament?

Perhaps models of sacrifice that live in healthier partnerships with our urgent sustainability needs are models that call people "to give up aspects of their lifestyles"[18] for the sake of the health and flourishing of earth and for the well-being of all people who live, work, and play in and on the soil of the earth. It takes life—the sacrifice of some elements of life—to sustain life. How in our faith communities can we invite Lament to sing her soul-sustaining elegies, to guide us to mourn both the acknowledged and too often unacknowledged sacrifices that make possible our everyday lives?

The communal dimension of lament is important again here. To be aware of all that it takes in terms of the earth's resources and the labor of some workers to sustain my personal everyday life, not to

---

[17] Christopher Key Chapple, "Sacrifice and Sustainability" (2008), *Theological Studies Faculty Works,* paper 20, http://digitalcommons.lmu.edu/theo_fac/20 (accessed October 25, 2016).

[18] Ibid.

mention our communal and societal lives, requires, as Chapple says, "connectivity with others and with the primary source of revelation, the earth community." [19] Seth Stevenson of *Slate* magazine speaks to this by filling in the MasterCard ad meme with these provocative words: "Mind-blowing realization that our daily lives both intertwine with and enable a shadow-world built on oil, illicit drugs, and clandestine diplomacy-by-violence: Priceless." [20]

How do issues of production, costs, and advertising relate to Christian liturgies? The bread of our Lord's meal celebrations comes to mind. In our liturgies at the sacred table, we reverence bread for the spiritual and theological ways it makes real in our lives the story of Jesus' life, death, and resurrection. We remember and grieve Jesus' death even as we celebrate that this death—this sacrifice—in mysterious ways beyond human comprehension resulted in life renewed and sustained. Embedded in this story is the reality that it takes life to sustain life.

How is Lament present when we take, break, bless, and eat the bread of life at the Lord's table? At this table, do we lament that we live in a world even now where God's beloved child could be (and in some cases is) murdered for the sake of political gain? At this table do we lament the sacrifices of time and labor of farmers and fieldworkers that are mixed into the ingredients of the bread of life? At this table do we lament the sacrifices of the earth—of God's good humus—that make possible this bread of life? And do we lament at this table our own fragility? Do we lament that we are earth and to earth we shall return in this great cycle of life and death?

[19] Ibid.

[20] Seth Stevenson, "The End of a Played-Out Ad Campaign?" *Slate*, March 13, 2006, http://www.slate.com/articles/business/ad_report_card/2006/03/the_end_of_a_playedout_ad_campaign.html.

Death, grief, and lament are an ever-present trio in the song of life. Communities of faith need to tune their ears more often and with greater reverence at the Lord's table and in other parts of our liturgies to the aching tones and textures of each in people's lives. We need to tune our ears in our worship to the realities of human fragility and the precariousness of human life.

Samuel Proctor names human fragility as a primary basis for human community:

> [Community] begins with biology, for we all have a common origin and share the same biological equipment, possibilities, and limitations. Some of us may be wealthy and some even of royal birth, but at bottom we are made of the same stuff and have more in common than what separates us. We also have a common dependence on the physical resources of the planet. . . Further, we share the same destiny. After three score years and ten, life gets precarious for everyone, and our days are numbered. Soon we all "take our chambers in the silent halls of death," and this reminds us of our commonality. No matter how much we leave or what is spent on our funerals, we are permanently removed, and this frame of clay returns, ashes to ashes, dust to dust, and earth to earth. [21]

We are better able to discern with wisdom what we wish to sustain when we begin or at least keep in mind our shared human fragilities, dependencies, and limitations.

What are some concrete ways communities can tune their ears to and join their voices with Lament's voice in their liturgies?

First, communities can seek to balance in weekly worship expressions of praise and celebration with times for open-ended vocalizations of grief and despair and even of complaint against God; balance

---

[21] Proctor, *Certain Sound of the Trumpet*, 15.

can be achieved through music, prayers, and readings of psalms of lament and through other liturgical actions that speak to or embody painful truths about human life. Important to remember when crafting prayers of lament is that while Lament mourns, the act of lament itself is also an act of communal proclamation of Gospel truths.[22]

In places where individuals are free to bring to worship their stories of suffering and loss, they discover a cloud of witnesses, a community of people who acknowledge their pain and stand with them in that pain without urging or expecting resolution that looks or sounds a certain way or that fits within a certain time frame. Common ritual responses to the death of a loved one such as "She's in a better place" or "God doesn't give us more than we can bear" are replaced in communities of shared lament by attentive listening as people proclaim, with as much fervor and raw truth as a prophet, the depth and inconsolability of their anguish and thus the pain and fragility of their humanity.

Looking into the face of grief, beholding the rage of one whose heart is shattered or whose body has been razed by rape or disease or injury, can be a terrifying prospect because it causes us to look at the reality of our own mortality.[23] But to make room for full-bodied expressions of pain and grief is to embody faith's most radical dimension. To embody lament as a community is to proclaim in the face of the worst of what life can dole out that nothing is too painful or difficult or terrifying to bring before God in the sacred space of communal worship and prayer. When we can say or embody or sing or pray or cry out in worship the full range of what we feel in the depths of our bones, then over time, even if only in incremental slivers, perhaps we will risk releasing all of it into the hope of God's grace.

[22] Sally A. Brown and Patrick D. Miller, "Introduction" in *Lament: Proclaiming Practices in Pulpit, Pew and Public Square,* ed. Brown and Miller (Philadelphia: Westminster/John Knox, 2005), xv.

[23] Ellington, *Risking Truth*, 8.

When communities embody authentic lament in their liturgies, the healing power of that lament moves out across worship's threshold into everyday life. Similar to other elements of worship, lament arises from and returns to the places where people live and work. Lament is birthed in and returns to the places where violence slashes bodies and devastates the earth. And the promise of the Gospel is that we can discover divine epiphanies in the everyday places where Lament lives. After all, Lament herself bears in her face, even in her very soul, the image of God.

The naturalist Henry Breston expresses this insight in a unique way. Breston spent a year in the late 1920s living in a small house he built on Cape Cod's outer beach. Each day he sat at his kitchen table and recorded his thoughts and observations as he looked out on the restless ocean tides. Breston sees and hears in the daily rhythms of beach and sea deep truths about life. He writes, for example, about how during a winter storm, the skeleton of a ship buried for over a century in a dune "floated and lifted itself free, thus stirring from its grave and yielding its bones again to the fury of the gale." [24]

Perhaps Breston names something here about last year's nests. In this world Breston inhabits, Robert Finch says in his introduction to Breston's memoir, "[L]ife and death are constantly changing and inter-changeable." We see the truth of this only in scraps and moments in the book, but in Breston's writing, "incidents small and fragmentary take on sharp, but momentary, identity and significance." [25] The significance of the momentary lingers even as the shore constantly shifts and changes.

Perhaps God sustains the earth and human communities through life's fragmentary incidents as much as through mighty acts in his-

---

[24] Henry Beston, *The Outermost House: A Year of Life on the Great Beach of Cape Cod* (New York: St. Martin's Griffin, 1949), 135.

[25] Robert Finch, "Introduction," in Henry Beston, *The Outermost House: A Year of Life on the Great Beach of Cape Cod* (New York: St. Martin's Griffin, 1949), xi–xxxii.

tory. When we can name in our worship the many and unrelenting ways skeletons—those things long buried and those things too often neglected or forgotten—yield their bones again and again to the fury of life's gale, perhaps we draw closer to the truth of our humanity.

Breston's words about the century-old ship's skeleton in a winter sea are haunting. They conjure for me images of slave ships moving through the Middle Passage and the lives that were lost in those wintry waters—lives never mourned, lives forgotten. Images come to mind too of floods in Louisiana that have washed away homes and businesses and that have buried dreams. What winter liturgies can we cultivate in our worship to make space for those skeletons that remind us of the horrors humans can do to one another or of the tragedies left in the wake of natural disasters? How can our prayers or songs or sermons set the truths of those realities free so that their bones again prophesy to us and renovate and redeem our perceptions of ourselves, our world, and our futures? Ezekiel's valley-scattered dry bones come to mind:

> Then the guide said to me, "Prophesy to these bones, and say to them: O dry bones, hear the word of the Lord. Thus says the Lord God to these bones: I will cause breath to enter you, and you shall live. I will lay sinews on you, and will cause flesh to come upon you, and cover you with skin, and put breath in you, and you shall live; and you shall know that I am the Lord." So I prophesied as I had been commanded; and as I prophesied, suddenly there was a noise, a rattling, and the bones came together, bone to its bone. I looked, and there were sinews on them, and flesh had come upon them, and skin had covered them; but there was no breath in them. Then God said to me, "Prophesy to the breath, prophesy, mortal, and say to the breath: Thus says the Lord God: Come from the four winds, O breath, and breathe upon these slain, that they may live." I prophesied as he commanded me, and the breath came

into them, and they lived, and stood on their feet, a vast multi-
tude. Then he said to me, "Mortal, these bones are the whole
house of Israel. They say, 'Our bones are dried up, and our
hope is lost; we are cut off completely.' Therefore prophesy,
and say to them, Thus says the Lord God: I am going to open
your graves, and bring you up from your graves, O my people;
and I will bring you back to the land of Israel. And you shall
know that I am the Lord, when I open your graves, and bring
you up from your graves, O my people. I will put my spirit
within you, and you shall live, and I will place you on your
own soil; then you shall know that I, the Lord, have spoken
and will act," says the Lord. (Ezek 4:4-14)

Striking about this image from the ancient prophet is that all the bones
stir up out of the dust to live again, not just the ones whose lives have
been beloved and grieved. Rising up out of Ezekiel's dry bones valley
are all the skeletons that haunt our landscapes, perhaps especially
those we would just as soon forget but that in vital ways stir us to
authentic confession and lamentation.

That, again, is the wonder and terror of Praise and Lament's inexo-
rable shared dance. As Breston writes, life and death are obstinately
interchangeable. This means that when we embrace and celebrate life,
whether we acknowledge it or not, we also embrace death. Lament
lives in our cities alongside Praise. Both should also be given space
to move and speak in our worship.

The Enduring Thread of Last Year's Nest

Perhaps the old nest I rescued that rainy spring day holds wisdom for the challenges that Christian communities face today as we
struggle to discern what it is we want and need to sustain about our
identities and our worship. When I returned home in the afternoon
after rescuing the abandoned nest, I photographed it.

The next day I decided to take a few more photos. But the nest was no longer where I had left it. I wondered if perhaps another critter had taken it or even another person. Then I noticed that the nest was about halfway up the sidewalk toward my house. The wind was the culprit perhaps? The next day, the nest was even closer to the house. I noticed that it was smaller too.

Looking at my photographs later that evening, a flash of sapphire caught my eye. Last year's birds had somewhere found a leftover piece of yarn, perhaps from a sweater or afghan, to thread into the dwelling where they would hatch that year's nestlings. That was when I realized this year's birds were using bits and pieces of last year's nest to build for this spring season. At least, that is what I imagined. Another image from Ezekiel surfaced for me as I reflected on last year's nest:

> Thus says the Lord God:
> I myself will take a sprig
> > from the lofty top of a cedar;
> > I will set it out.
> I will break off a tender one
> > from the topmost of its young twigs;
> I myself will plant it
> > on a high and lofty mountain.
> > On the mountain height of Israel
> > I will plant it,
> in order that it may produce boughs and bear fruit,
> > and become a noble cedar.
> Under it every kind of bird will live;
> > in the shade of its branches will nest
> > winged creatures of every kind.
> > All the trees of the field shall know
> > that I am the Lord.
> I bring low the high tree,
> > I make high the low tree;

I dry up the green tree
and make the dry tree flourish.
I the Lord have spoken;
I will accomplish it. (Ezek 17:22-24)

Is that Lament's invitation—to the idea that God sustains the earth and communities of faith by fashioning a dwelling place where winged creatures of every kind can live and thrive?

Perhaps that is how Lament joins us in our work to sustain those things about human communities that are life-giving and grace-filled. She points toward those choice twigs and bits of sapphire yarn from last year's nest that remind present and future nestlings of the gifts and challenges of the past and urges us to make the nests we are building now places birds of every kind can call home.

Interlude

Answered Prayer[1]

Dr. William Barber II is one of my heroes. He wrote an op-ed titled "Prophetic Moral Challenge after the National Prayer Breakfast" following the 2017 National Prayer Breakfast. I have continued to think about his essay and about the powerful words he quoted from Frederick Douglass (1818–1895): "I prayed for freedom for twenty years but received no answer until I prayed with my legs."[2]

> "These times we're living in
> call for courageous people,"
> the preacher said that day.

> I am not brave.
> Never have been.
> Bravery is something to be
> read about in storybooks
> where quixotic heroes
> ride out on prancing
> stallions to do battle,
> sabers flashing in
> magnificent sunlight.

[1] A version of this reflection first appeared as Jill Crainshaw, "Answered Prayer," *Unfundamentalist Christians*, February 5, 2017, www.patheos.com /blogs/unfundamentalistchristians/2017/02/answered-prayer/ (accessed June 9, 2017).

[2] William J. Barber II, "OpEd: Prophetic Moral Challenge after the National Prayer Breakfast," *NBCNews.com*, NBCUniversal News Group, February 3, 2017, www.nbcnews.com/news/nbcblk/oped-moral-outrage-after-national -prayer-breakfast-n716261 (accessed June 9, 2017).

Bravery is something to be
prayed for in church
where harsh living
daylights must first pass
by saintly stained-glass
sentinels of bygone years
before being transmuted
into the kinder, gentler
beams that caress Sunday
morning's bowed heads.

But maybe we should
pray for freedom,
like Frederick Douglass did,
and then walk in faith
until our legs are braver
than our thoughts.

So, in this present cloud
of unknowing, being not
brave, we resolve, if
we can find the honesty
to do it, to live on
as best we can,
stringing together each
momentary breath
like pearls of hope to
place with the gentleness
of a lover around our
fear to name its wounds
as our own and journey on
not in spite of
but with it.

For out there, where the
times we're living in
call for courageous people,
the groaning ground that
soaked up the life-blood of
all who died unjustly just
trying to live
needs the redeeming touch
of feet determined to walk
with their fear until
their legs have learned
to move each day to the
rhythms of justice,
mercy, and love.

Chapter 7

We Never Made It to Thank You

Two are better than one, because they have a good reward for
their toil. For if they fall, one will lift up the other; but woe to one
who is alone and falls and does not have another to help. Again,
if two lie together, they keep warm; but how can one keep warm
alone? And though one might prevail against another, two will
withstand one. A threefold cord is not quickly broken.

—Ecclesiastes 4:9-12

What do you say when someone gives you a gift? Most people
know the answer. Or they think they do. We have known it since childhood. Possibly learned it at a young age from an etiquette-conscious
adult. The answer is part of a common ritual. Someone gives you a
gift, and you say, "Thank you."

But Thomas had a different response in mind during the moment
for children at my church one Sunday several years ago. On that
Sunday, his mouth moved as fast as his feet as he ran to the front of
the sanctuary. The leader talked about birthday parties. "What do
you like about birthday parties?"

"Cake!" Thomas shouted.

"Balloons?" Rhonda asked. She was timid.

One child offered the magic answer: "Presents!"

That was the leader's signal to ask a second question. "What do you say when someone gives you a present and you unwrap it?" She held up a package wrapped in colorful paper and tied up with a bow.

I suspect an answer scurried to the tips of the tongues of just about every adult gathered for worship that day. I smiled. The leader was doing a nice job with this lesson on expressing gratitude.

But then Thomas prophesied. He witnessed. He blurted out what his young heart could not contain.

"What do you say when someone gives you a gift?" the leader asked.

Instead of speaking words, Thomas gasped and then "oohed."

I laughed along with others in the sanctuary, but our laughter was the caught-off-guard laughter of worshipers made wiser by a child's insight.

"What is the second thing you say?" the leader asked. Perhaps she still hoped to get to where she'd imagined the children's moment would go that day. But now the children were in sync with each other and with God's spirit dancing in our midst.

"What is the second thing you say?"

"Wow!" Rhonda exclaimed. She was not so timid now.

I don't recall how that moment with the children ended. I do recall that though the worship service continued on its usual course, Thomas, Rhonda, and the others had invited me down a road that was anything but usual. Thomas did not respond to the leader's questions as one schooled in gift-receiving etiquette. Rhonda did not respond based on whether or not the colorful wrapping of the package the leader had with her contained a longed-for gift. They never even opened the package. The children's responses in worship that day bubbled up out of anticipated possibilities of gift-giving and receiving. Their responses surged up from a place of an expectation of delight. They expected to be wowed by a gift that had not yet been unwrapped.

Someone joked after church: "Well, the children never made it to 'thank you.'"

The assessment was accurate, and I was glad, for instead of repeating the familiar mantra of "thank you," we plunged into less known, potentially life-altering depths of unqualified, even disruptive delight.

I shared this memory in a keynote address at the 2014 Faith and Health Summit sponsored by the North Carolina Council of Churches. The event brought together pastoral and lay leaders, lawmakers, public health professionals, and other community members to explore connections between faith and public health. The summit emerged out of the council's Partners for Wholeness and Health program, an initiative designed to "support places of worship in their efforts to create healthy and whole congregants by connecting them with quality health programs and resources in the community."[1]

The program's emphasis on linking worshiping communities and public health resources is striking and is one of the gifts the North Carolina Council of Churches offers to faith communities and to the public square. The council makes its home "at the intersection of faith, social justice and policy" in North Carolina with the goal of enabling "denominations, congregations, and people of faith to individually and collectively impact our state on issues such as economic justice and development, human well-being, equality, compassion and peace, following the example and mission of Jesus Christ."[2] The council is interested in the links between the worship of faith communities and the work those same communities do to respond to the problems and challenges present in their neighborhoods and cities.

---

[1] Partners for Wholeness and Health, http://www.ncchurches.org/programs/health-wholeness/ (accessed October 26, 2016).

[2] From the Council's Mission Statement, http://www.ncchurches.org/about/.

The question at the center of the 2014 Faith Health Summit asked what has become in our times a common wondering of faith communities and religious leaders: what can faith communities do to improve or shape public health and well-being?

Something about that question called to my mind Thomas's and Rhonda's responses during that moment for children in the worship service at my church: *authentic expectations of delight.* What if *this* concept—the concept embedded in the children's liturgical "oohs" and "wows" blurted out before the gift was even unwrapped—what if this is what faith communities can contribute to the work in neighborhoods and cities to respond to exorbitant health-care costs, health insurance challenges and injustices, and issues of food insecurity? What if we as communities of worship can encourage civic and business leaders to consider a different starting place for their conversations when they gather around public decision-making tables? What if we invite them to begin with expectations of delight as they face formidable and seemingly intractable public health problems?

Of course, this is not the usual way most of us approach societal challenges. When I enter into discussions about health-care costs and inequities, I don't enter into them with expectations of delight. I am more likely to show up at those conversation tables with my critical thinking apparatus fired up, my problem-solving skills in hand, and my sharp rebuttals on standby. I often enter into these conversations anticipating a debate or expecting workable solutions to be hard to come by.

But what if communities of faith and pastoral leaders offer *this* gift to these discussions: a mysterious—even quirky and stubborn capacity to begin with possibilities instead of problems. To look for abundances instead of deficiencies. [3]

---

[3] See Peter Block, *Community: The Structure of Belonging* (San Francisco: Berrett-Koehler Publishers, 2009).

Some may worry that such an approach is unrealistic or not critical enough of the systemic structures and powers that lead to discrimination, poverty, racism, gender inequities, and other public problems. Others may argue that a focus on delight is a luxury not yet available to communities where people's lives are at risk every day.

But theological delight is more than a luxury. Delight emerges out of embodied participation in justice and community making. This means delight is vital to public transformation. Liturgical theologian Nicholas Westerhoff says this about delight, community, and shalom: "A community of shalom, for one thing, is a responsible community: where shalom exists, there we enact our responsibilities to one another, to God, and to nature. But shalom is more than that. It is fully present only where there is delight and joy in those relationships."[4]

Perhaps this is another way to express the role of delight in the work we undertake to restore and create equitable structures of public health: faith communities bring to the work we all must do to resolve public problems a unique capacity to cultivate everyday wonder and delight as a life-altering, relationship-building dimension of justice making and policy transforming.

An Unexpected Dialogue Partner

The Faith Health Summit planners that year asked me to speak on the theme "We're Better Together." The text they chose for the day's theme was Ecclesiastes 4:9-10a: "Two are better than one, because they have a good reward for their toil. For if they fall, one will lift up the other."

When I learned what the theme was to be, I recalled the primary aim of Partners in Health and Wholeness—to build partnerships between faith communities and local health programs and providers.

---

[4] Nicholas Westerhoff, *Until Justice and Peace Embrace: The Kuyper Lectures for 1981 Delivered at the Free University of Amsterdam* (Grand Rapids, MI: Eerdmans, 1983), 124.

The idea that individuals, churches, and health programs cannot succeed in isolation from one another is central both to the highlighted Ecclesiastes verses and to the mission of Partners in Health and Wholeness. Relationships are also central to cultivating delight.

But what makes the Ecclesiastes writer an unexpected dialogue partner for Partners in Health and Wholeness is that this ancient thinker and writer was a skeptic and a cynic whereas the leaders and communities connected to Partners in Health and Wholeness have invested their energies in the possibilities of communal partnerships. I have experienced the leaders of Partners in Health and wholeness to be hopeful optimists. The Ecclesiastes writer seems to be the opposite of that.

Who was this ancient cynic? "Ecclesiastes" is a Greek term for the Hebrew "Qoheleth," which means the gatherer or the assembler. Traditionally, the word "Qoheleth" has been translated teacher or preacher. Qoheleth was a product of his time. Many scholars believe that the book of Ecclesiastes emerged out of a time of socioeconomic upheaval in the ancient Near Eastern world. Qoheleth lived in an age of disillusionment when the once-revered wisdom of the past no longer seemed relevant or useful, and he bemoans in his writings the endlessness of work and the seeming meaninglessness of life.[5]

Qoheleth was not a cheerful preacher. Biblical scholar William P. Brown highlights Qoheleth's "unflinchingly realistic perspectives on the value of life."[6] Qoheleth looked around his city at the realities of human toil and eventual death and concluded that life on the whole is "vanity." Life is fragile and futile, and in the midst of it God is unreadable and unknowable. More than thirty-five times in Ecclesiastes, Qoheleth says that life is vanity.[7]

---

[5] William P. Brown (*Ecclesiastes* [Louisville, KY: Westminster John Knox Press, 2011]), 8, argues for dating Ecclesiastes in the Persian/early Hellenistic period.
[6] Ibid., 9.
[7] Ibid.

Qoheleth's groans of existential weariness are familiar to people today who work hard to repair or change broken political, economic, or health systems. A colleague who works in public health has said to me on more than one occasion something like this: "I feel like we just keep having the same conversations over and over again about health insurance costs, disease prevention, sanitation, clean water, and other issues related to human flourishing and well-being. I don't understand why we seem to make such little progress. I have spent my adult life doing this work and advocating for change, and I wonder sometimes what difference I have made."

My colleague is not alone in her feelings of ineffectiveness. Indeed, much of what we hear about and see in the news can persuade us that our work to change unjust structures or repair fractured health, economic, or political systems is in vain. The powers that be are too entrenched and the problems too massive. Qoheleth's ancient sigh is recognizable to many people today.

But then, in Ecclesiastes 4, this bleak-spirited preacher looks out over his neighborhood and glimpses something surprising and perhaps even hopeful out of the corner of his eye, an enigma in the midst of the endless and futile repetitions of human affairs. He proclaims with unexpected delight: "Two are better than one."

What does Qoheleth see that enlivens his eyes and his heart, if but for a moment? The scene does not include enough detail for us to know for certain, but we do encounter here Qoheleth doing what he does throughout the book. He observes "life under the sun" and then rouses the imaginations of his readers by using poems, proverbs, stories, images, and metaphors to depict what he sees and to illustrate what wisdom he gleans from what he sees.[8]

---

[8] Eunny P. Lee, *The Vitality of Enjoyment in Qohelet's Theological Rhetoric,* BZAW 353 (Berlin: Walter de Gruyter, 2005), 127.

The verses that lead up to those emphasized by the Faith Health Summit expand this unexpected proclamation that two are better than one:

> Again I saw all the oppressions that are practiced under the sun. Look, the tears of the oppressed—with no one to comfort them! On the side of their oppressors there was power—with no one to comfort them. And I thought the dead, who have already died, more fortunate than the living, who are still alive; but better than both is the one who has not yet been, and has not seen the evil deeds that are done under the sun.
>
> Then I saw that all toil and all skill in work come from one person's envy of another. This also is vanity and a chasing after wind.
>
> Fools fold their hands
> and consume their own flesh.
> Better is a handful with quiet
> than two handfuls with toil,
> and a chasing after wind.
>
> Again, I saw vanity under the sun: the case of solitary individuals, without sons or brothers; yet there is no end to all their toil, and their eyes are never satisfied with riches. "For whom am I toiling," they ask, "and depriving myself of pleasure?" This also is vanity and an unhappy business.
>
> Two are better than one, because they have a good reward for their toil. For if they fall, one will lift up the other; but woe to one who is alone and falls and does not have another to help. Again, if two lie together, they keep warm; but how can one keep warm alone? And though one might prevail against another, two will withstand one. A threefold cord is not quickly broken. (Eccl 4:1-12)

Qoheleth's concluding words in these chapters—"two are better than one"—were the delightful surprise that captured the imaginations of the planners of the summit.

What did they hear in this ancient text? When we work together in community, we are stronger. We are more insightful. We are more likely to withstand dangers. We are more likely to bring about needed changes for our communities.

Gary Gunderson, leader of the Faith and Health Ministries division at Wake Forest University Baptist Medical Center, echoes both Qoheleth and the summit theme with his insights about how faith communities contribute to public health and vitality:

> Those looking for magical or remote actions of God and those looking for functional techniques of healthcare or disease prevention are both missing the most vital and interesting contribution of faith. It creates webs of relationship that can add efficiency to many human systems and also add intelligence and creativity that allows systems to break through into other possibilities. [9]

Gunderson speaks with confidence about the "revolutionary effect of webs of trust" on how public health functions. Webs of trust, he writes, do "not just ameliorate disease but actually improve health." [10]

The idea of connectedness is at the core of Christian faith. God's people at worship and at work are the Body of Christ. Sacred connectional tissue binds us together and life-giving blood formed in the marrow of our bones flows through us as God's Body so that each part—each member—belongs to the other (Rom 12:5; 1 Cor 12:27). To

---

[9] Gary Gunderson, "Faith, Health, and the Vitality of the Church, *Ecclesio. com*, June 22, 2011, http://www.ecclesio.com/2011/06/faith-health-and-the-vitality-of-the-church-by-gary-gunderson/ (accessed October 26, 2016).

[10] Ibid.

recognize and relish this connectedness—this web of people "made into one by God's action"—is to cultivate the surprise of delight and hope in the midst of difficult challenges and even to spark transformation of unhealthy systems and structures such as politics, economics, education, and health in our tangled public worlds. [11]

Gunderson witnessed this delight firsthand through what is now referred to as the "Memphis Model." In 2005, while senior vice president at Methodist LeBonheur Healthcare, Gunderson and a group of health-care and congregational partners developed a holistic health-care strategy that utilized congregations working together with health navigators to do public health outreach in Memphis communities. A central aim of the Memphis Model is to create partnerships of trust and then to spin out from those partnerships relational webs and strategies for mapping health assets and building communities' health capacities. [12] The success of the Memphis Model in Memphis is well-documented. In Memphis, long-broken bridges of trust between the hospital and surrounding communities are being rebuilt through the congregational health-care navigators partnerships. Positive outcomes for public heath have been significant. [13]

---

[11] Ibid.

[12] Mary Vanderslice, "Faith Filled and Healthy Communities: The Memphis Congregational Network," *The White House*, June 21, 2011, https://www.white house.gov/blog/2011/06/21/faith-filled-healthy-communities-memphis-congrega tional-health-network (accessed October 26, 2016).

[13] Alex Halperin, "It Really Does Take a Village: How Memphis Is Fixing Healthcare," *Salon.com*, September 3, 2013, http://www.salon.com/2013/09/03 /it_really_does_take_a_ village_how_memphis_is_fixing_healthcare/ (accessed October 26, 2016). "The data is impressive. Methodist says that CHN members, many of whom are living with chronic diseases, are staying in the hospital for less time since they enrolled and the cost of caring *for the same patients* has fallen since they joined the network. A study of CHN patients showed that after discharge, a group of them stayed out of the hospital for a median of 426 days compared with 306 days for patients not in the network, an improvement of almost 40 percent—hospital administrators are watching readmissions data closely

Speaking in a different time and place, Qoheleth arrives at a conclusion similar to Gunderson's: "Two are better than one"; "a threefold cord is not quickly broken." Qoheleth glimpses this wisdom in his time despite his cynical lens on life and the world. In the midst of humanity's weak substitutes for justice and proclivities to chase after the wind, in the midst of "all the oppressions that are practiced under the sun"—ahh—a glimpse of possibility; a three-stranded cord is not quickly broken. We have each other. We are stronger, warmer, less weary, more courageous together.

Biblical scholar Eunny P. Lee explores the relationship between Qoheleth's insistence on meaninglessness, his emphasis on enjoying life to the fullest, and his observation that "two are better than one":

> Vanity of vanities, says the Teacher,
> vanity of vanities! All is vanity.
> What do people gain from all the toil
> at which they toil under the sun? (Eccl 1:2-3)

> So I commend enjoyment, for there is nothing better for people under the sun than to eat, and drink, and enjoy themselves, for this will go with them in their toil through the days of life that God gives them under the sun. (Eccl 8:15)

How are these three connected, Lee asks? The surprise and the gift of Qoheleth's theology of work and delight, Lee determines, is its groundedness in a communal ethic. One of life's tragedies, Qoheleth laments in 4:9-12, is the isolation of weary individuals toiling away with no companion, with no one to comfort or care for them. [14] The

---

because the Affordable Care Act penalizes hospitals when patients are readmitted within 30 days. Over a three-year period, CHN members also had a significantly lower mortality rate. Methodist says CHN costs about $1 million per year to run, not including outside grants, and saves the hospital $4 million in annual costs."

[14] Eunny P. Lee, *The Vitality of Enjoyment*, 130.

absence of community sharpens even more the already whetted knife of oppression and deepens the ever-present absurdity of life. For Qoheleth, as Brown says, "the moral life is grounded in the responsible practice of enjoyment, that is, enjoyment that promotes not only the flourishing of the individual, but also the life of the larger human community." [15]

What kind of enjoyment promotes communal flourishing and what does it have to do with liturgical practices? Emphasized throughout Ecclesiastes are everyday activities that are also activities common to worship. Eating and drinking are highlighted in Ecclesiastes (2:24, 3:13, 8:15, 9:7). So, too are work and community (3:22, 9:7-10). As Brown says, "Qoheleth's taxonomy of joy includes not only the delights of basic sustenance ('eating' and 'drinking') but also of work and community." [16] Qoheleth looks realistically at those things about life that are futile and that lead to emptiness, things like chasing after wealth or fame or greediness, and he decides in the end to celebrate everyday life's most ordinary rhythms.

Worship also celebrates life's ordinary daily rhythms as sacred. For example, table fellowship, vital to everyday life, is central to Christian worship and, as Brown says, "has its own peculiar ethos." At the Lord's table in worship, "all self-striving is banished . . . [and] the fellowship and unity of the body—the church—is paramount." [17] What if worship's table ethos was our ethos for everyday table fellowship?

While not a New Testament text, Ecclesiastes too relishes the life-giving and joy-sustaining actions that are enlivened when people eat and drink together. Biblical scholar Elsa Tamez concludes this about Qoheleth's approach to the estranging and isolating absurdities of life: Qoheleth observes a world full of troubles—a "Hellenistic pro-

[15] Brown, *Ecclesiates*, 10.
[16] Ibid., 127.
[17] Ibid., 129.

duction system of enslaving toil"—and proposes an attitude toward life "that follows the heart and the eyes" and affirms the humanity of persons who live in this world. The way to affirm life is

> by eating bread and drinking wine with enjoyment, with the person one loves, and in the midst of enslaving toil. . . . Qoheleth works, acts, examines, reflects, seeks, and comes to the conclusion that there is nothing better than this everyday activity. . . . The utopia of everyday enjoyment is a viable, humanizing way of repudiating the present but at the same time living it by a contrary logic. That is, to live as human beings who feel that they are alive, in a society that does not allow them to live because of its demands for productivity and efficiency. [18]

Tamez emphasizes what is perhaps the most striking message of Qoheleth. The delight in life Qoheleth advocates does not ignore the fact that in the real world many are overwhelmed by feelings of helplessness or are oppressed by dominant economic and political policies. To eat and drink and enjoy life in a way that is indifferent to "the exploitation that takes place under the sun"[19] is also vanity. Indifference also leads to meaninglessness.

Qoheleth insists on embracing life's delight *"in the midst of the absurdity"*[20] as a radical communal stance of resistance. Qoheleth challenges the "logic of the absurdity of life by living by the logic of 'non-absurdity': by eating bread, drinking wine and enjoying life with a loved one."[21] Authentic life—real life—is to be found in eating bread and drinking wine in the company of people we love, in community.

---

[18]Elsa Tamez, *When the Horizons Close: Rereading Ecclesiastes* (Maryknoll, NY: Orbis Books, 2000), 25.

[19]Ibid., 30.

[20]Ibid., 27; emphasis added.

[21]Ibid.

This wisdom from Qoheleth is rich with insights for liturgical practices. In worship, when we eat and drink together at the Lord's table, we delight in gifts of God's creation. We delight in God's grace as it is taken into our bodies and souls in that very moment. We remember the hard realities of life as we eat and drink and remember the life and death of Jesus; we also anticipate that season when God will act with justice on behalf of all people. But we *live toward* that as yet unseen justice-infused season with an *expectation of delight* because we have decided to embody *in the present* a stance of radical communal resistance in the midst of life's injustices.

This is the peculiar gift Christian communities contribute to the work many people in cities and neighborhoods are doing to transform and renew public systems, policies, and practices of all kinds. At the Lord's table in worship, we delight together in the mysteries of God's bread and wine, and the meal changes us. At least, it can change us, if we open ourselves to it and to the people with whom we share it. Then, transformed, we eat and drink differently—with hearts, eyes, and spirits wider open and more hospitable—at our everyday dining tables. And we hear and speak differently—with more expansive compassion and a deeper sense of investment—at tables where conversations unfold about topics ranging from personal joys and sorrows to public health and economic issues to concerns about hunger and clean water access.

Most of the Faith Health Summit participants came to the event already knowing on some level that "two are better than one." The participants—health-care providers, caregivers, pastoral leaders, volunteers, and others—have been working, imagining, and working again for many years for healthy changes in their neighborhoods and cities, and they have seen that the problems our communities face are too big for one person or group to overcome alone. The participants came to a summit—a high-level place—to look out over their neighborhoods yet again, to dream one more time, to seek once more concrete ways to keep their work moving toward Qoheleth's wisdom.

Perhaps for those Faith Health Summit participants and for any of us who work to make a difference in the face of long-enduring societal problems, Qoheleth's wisdom emerges as the kind of question I posed in my comments that day. I looked out into those diverse faces and imagined the varied stories that brought them together on that day. One woman who sat near the front told me she is a nurse working with hospice; she spent many hours of her days wiping the sweat from the brows of patients dying with cancer. The man two rows in front of her is pastor of a small congregation in the city; his people live, work, and worship in a "food desert." On the front row was a college student, studying physical therapy at a local college. Next to her was a man who sat with a walker in the aisle beside him; he is a physician who had traveled many times to other countries to provide medical care.

Into the midst of these passionate, justice-seeking people, I offered a question that organizational development consultant Peter Block asks in his work. It is a question that I heard echoed in Ecclesiastes and in the children's time at my church and that I believe each Lord's Table gathering asks of us: "How will the world be different tomorrow as a result of our meeting today?"[22]

To ask this question is to spark the possibility of stepping into encounters and conversations with an authentic expectation of delight, with a belief or hope that together we can see at least a miniscule shift if not a significant revolution. When we come to the summit expecting delight, the usual strategies and even the usual language shifts because we gather with a belief that new ways of

[22] Block, *Community,* quotes Kathie Dannemiller, a corporate change consultant who worked with Ford Company leaders in the 1980s to create a process called "whole-scale change."

being and doing are present with us in the room, in the hearts, minds, ideas, and experiences of the people with whom we are gathered. Created in God's image, we bring possibilities with us through the door. To approach life with authentic expectations of delight means that we believe that the wisdom to weave our multiple strands of knowledge, passion, and experience together into an unbreakable cord resides in us, in the stories, faces, and lives of all who work and struggle and toil and work again day after day.

Spirituality of Disruption

Susan's physical therapist asked my community of faith to sing carols at Susan's house one Christmas. I agreed but I was reluctant. We did not need to stay long, I decided.

Susan is ten years old and faces many physical and cognitive challenges. She cannot walk or speak. "Susan loves music and makes sounds when she hears it," her mom said. "But we don't hear music in church very often. I worry that Susan will disrupt worship for others."

Our group sang. Susan, curled up on the floor, stirred but did not wake. It was time for us to go.

"Will you stay for tea?"

My usual response came to mind—"Thank you, but we don't want to trouble you."

The therapist disrupted my usual response before I could say it aloud: "If it's not too much trouble, we'd love to stay."

I sat. We sipped.

A phrase came to mind: spirituality of disruption. God's love disrupts the usual. I recalled a workshop on ministry and disabilities I had attended.

"I heard a Christmas song on the radio on my way here," a nurse said. "The one that says something like 'Til the soul feels its worth.' What else is the church to do if not to look into the faces of people—to take a stance of holiness with them until every soul feels its worth? When we open ourselves to other souls—this is how we value them."

The song the nurse had heard was "O Holy Night." The lyrics also say this: "Long lay the world"—not just individuals—but this whole aching earth of ours—"in sin and error *pining.* Til love appeared and the soul—felt its worth."

We didn't sing "O Holy Night" for Susan that day, but the song's spirit stirred for me in those moments when I stayed longer than I had planned. With teacups empty, we put on our coats. Then, just before we left, the physical therapist dropped to her knees next to Susan—an action I suppose she takes in her work over and over again day after day. Susan stirred at the sound of the therapist's voice: "Can I have a hug?"

Susan reached up; the therapist reached out; Susan's "oohhh" rang out. And I had the clear sense that for an instant, every soul in the room felt its worth. Perhaps, for a moment, the soul of the earth too was soothed. We had been visited by authentic delight.

Delight—the kind modeled and embodied in worship at the Lord's meal—invites a shift, away from efficiency and problem solving to profundity and connectivity, from a focus on mere improvements to a belief and insistence in ground-shifting change. We never made it to thank you at church on Sunday. I never said thank you aloud in Susan's house. Usual ways and responses were disrupted by something so ordinary it became the most profound thing in the room. We never made it to thank you. Instead we got to where redeeming work begins each day as we go out to our work and labor until evening—an authentic and radical expectation of delight.

Perhaps that is a worthy starting place for the work we need to incarnate in our bodies and as the Body of Christ today.

Interlude

Abide
A Sermon for an Ordination

Amy, a Baptist minister, was ordained in 2014 and installed as associate pastor of a Baptist church.[1] She asked me to preach the sermon for her ordination service. She chose as the text for the sermon and for the service as a whole John 15:1-7. When I asked Amy why she chose this text, not a conventional choice for an ordination sermon, she said:

> As a woman and a Baptist, I am committed to transforming hierarchy into relationships with friendship as the foundation. We do this work [of ministry] together connected to many who have come before me and many who will come after me. Ordination can tend to focus on the individual. I want to emphasize how the individual is part of a much larger whole.

Without realizing it, by adopting this perspective on ordination and ministry, Amy joined her voice to Qoheleth's and to contemporary justice seekers who see links between authentic, Gospel-forged friendship and transformation of unjust societal systems.

What is striking about Amy's perspective on ordination in conversation with John 15 is the link she sees between abiding and bearing fruit. Vital to productivity—to bearing fruit in ministry—is cultivating the wisdom to abide in God's grace and love.

[1] For a more extensive reflection on Amy's ordination rite, see Jill Crainshaw, "*They Spin with Their Hands*": *Women's Ordination Rites Renewing God's Work with God's People* (Ashland City, TN: OSL Press, 2015).

Paired together, abiding and fruit bearing become powerful and prophetic partners in cultivating friendships that "give love freely and generously without counting the cost and without wondering and worrying about who is on the receiving end of our limitless love."[2]

I sought in the ordination sermon that follows to capture Amy's perspective and link it both to ministry and everyday life. In John 15, Jesus distills spiritual wisdom from everyday life. The sermon connects that wisdom to religious leadership, ministry, and communal life.

Abide: A Sermon

"Abide in me as I abide in you" (John 15:4).

What kind of tree is he growing? Apple? Yes, there are apple blossoms, but I see pear blossoms too. And peach. The tree he is growing has been called "the tree of forty fruit." Forty *kinds* of fruit on one tree? I can't get my apple tree to bear—well, to bear apples! But artist Sam Van Aken grafts peach, pear, apricot, and apple branches onto a single root. He wants to preserve heirloom varieties and to resist fruit tree monocultures. "I want the tree of 40 fruit to interrupt the everyday," he says, "to change how people perceive life." And the tree grows! It bears fruit.[3]

Van Aken's tree—an abiding place—home—for forty kinds of fruit.

---

[2] Gail R. O'Day, "I Have Called You Friends," *Center for Ethics at Baylor University: The Christian Reflection Project*, 2008, http://www.baylor.edu/content /services/ document.php/61118.pdf (accessed October 26, 2016).

[3] See http://www.treeof40fruit.com/ (accessed October 26, 2016). See also Lauren Salked, "The Tree of 40 Fruit Is Exactly as Awesome as It Sounds," *Epicurious.com*, http://www.epicurious.com/archive/chefsexperts/interviews /sam-van-aken-interview (accessed October 26, 2016).

The Gospel of John's vine—an abiding place—home—for us, God's people.

How many of us know people who long for home? Maybe the longing enfolds them because they got lost from home and cannot find a way back. Or maybe longing comes to dwell in their hearts because they have only ever had a house—not a home—to reside in. Or perhaps something about home has changed both home and them. Jesus' words to his disciples are for people who long for home: I am your vine. I have made my home in, with, through, and all around you. I am that tree of forty fruit; each of you can find life with me. Abide in me. Dwell. Remain. Endure. Abide. In me.

So, there it is, Amy. Your calling. One word. Abide. That's it.

But we keep reading, and those red-letter words of Jesus complicate what at first sounds rather plain and simple. At least, that is what happened for me as I prepared for this sermon. I read this text and found myself getting all tangled up in the deeper meanings of what Jesus told his disciples on that long-ago night after dinner. When their bellies were full and they were "at home" with Jesus and each other. Before they went out to Gethsemane and every dream they had planted about who Jesus was and what that could mean for the future was cut down, chopped up, burned away. Before Jesus was killed and the memory of him began to haunt their nights and appear like a mirage in their days. Before they had plunged the depths of what homesickness can be in a human life when death and violence steal "home" away.

This homesickness is the soil of this text. The tangled meanings of the text grow up out of this soil to call to us, to call to you today, Amy, as you are ordained. Indeed, perhaps this is what John 15 calls us to do as ministers and as communities: to let ourselves get tangled up in a God-gifted life more complex and messy than we ever wanted it to be—and more life-giving than we have yet imagined it to be. ·

I like what Lutheran preacher Nadia Bolz Weber says about John 15: "So Jesus . . . can I be something a little more distinct? Perhaps you are the soil and I am the sunflower? Big, bright, audacious and distinctive."[4]

But this is not what we get in John. Tangled vines. Indistinguishable branches.[5] Always needing to be pruned and loved into life, not once but again and again.

And Jesus says we are to abide in him in this tangledness. That may be the hardest thing about this text. One challenge is the word "abide." Who uses that word today? Usage of "abide" spikes on a Google Ngram in 1840 and goes downhill from there. As Sheryl Kester-Byer says in her blog about this text, "Hotel signs don't say "come abide with us."[6] A spouse doesn't say on a wedding anniversary: "Honey, I'm glad we have abidden together all these years." "Abide" is a rare word—perhaps because the experience of abiding is rare.[7]

It is not like producing fruit. We can wrap our mathematical heads and busy hands around that. We can count blueberries and bunches of grapes. We can calculate salaries by the dollars per hour. We can quantify church growth by the number of new members per year. Amy, you can report how many programs you led or meetings you attended over a year in ministry. How much. How many. We know about that. We know how to rate

---

[4] Nadia Bolz Weber, "I Want to Be a Sunflower for Jesus," *The Hardest Question*, April 30, 2012, http://thq.wearesparkhouse.org/yearb/easter5gospe/ (accessed October 26, 2016).

[5] Ibid.

[6] Sheryl Kester-Byer, "Abiding," *Calvary Lutheran Church, Scotts Bluff, NE*, April 30, 2015, http://www.calvarylutheranscottsbluff.org/ps-my-spiritual -musings/abiding (accessed October 26, 2016).

[7] F. Dean Lueking, "Abide in Me . . . (John 15:1-8)," *Christian Century* (April 16, 1997): 387.

and adulate productivity. And we know something about cutting off or burning away whatever or whomever does not produce in the ways we think they should.[8]

But this Jesus who had no place to lay his head—Jesus calls us first and foremost to abide. Stay. Dwell. Be at home in God's love. And to hear this call changes all we think we know about Christian life and ministry. Ministry is not about producing. It is about abiding. We abide in love—grafted onto God's vine—*then* God's fierce gentleness cultivates fruit in us. And not fruit that all tastes or smells or looks the same. We are not all apples. We are peaches, apricots, and pluots. And we are all weighing down the branches of the same tree together.

Notice the plural pronouns in these verses. WE are all grafted onto the same tree. WE abide in God's love. WE bear fruit. This is not your ordinary tree, this fruit-bearing enigma that is God's called and beloved community.

To say "yes" to abiding is vital for today's church. And it is vital for you as a minister, Amy. Neither the church nor church ministers can compete on corporate productivity scales—not that we ever should have. Jesus calls us to bear something far more radical anyway. Jesus calls the church to create home—welcoming, nonjudging—for all kinds of people who seek God's staying places of justice, grace, and peace. Jesus doesn't ask us to cut, bind, burn, fix, control, enroll, or convince people but to befriend and love them. And even more radical, to let them call us out of our monoculture prisons to make home with them in multiblossomed, grace-infused love.

---

[8] Michael K. Marsh, "The Fruitfulness of Staying Connected—A Sermon on John 15:1-8, Easter 5B," *Interrupting the Silence*, May 7, 2012, interrupting thesilence.com/2012/05/07/the-fruitfulness-of-staying-connected-a-sermon -on-john-151-8-easter-5b/ (accessed June 9, 2017).

But what does it mean, in more concrete terms, for us to abide? A scene from the movie *Shall We Dance* comes to mind for me. In the movie, successful lawyer John Clark becomes restless in his life. He senses something is missing. Clark's imagination and energy are renewed when he secretly begins taking ballroom dance lessons.

Clark's wife grows suspicious. In a conversation with the private detective she hires, Clark's wife says this about marriage:

> We need a witness to our lives. There's a billion people on the planet. What does any one life really mean? But in a marriage, you're promising to care about everything. The good things, the bad things, the terrible things, the mundane things, all of it, all of the time, every day. You're saying, "Your life will not go unnoticed because I will notice it. Your life will not go unwitnessed because I will be your witness."[9]

This wisdom rings true for relationships in Christian communities too. We are called to bear witness to each other's lives, to acknowledge that we exist, to see and hear and care about each other. This is a vital part of what it means to abide with each other in God's gracious presence.

Amy, you say "yes" today to this call to bear witness in and with this beloved community. And they "say" yes to be a witness to your life. That calling invites us into the life-giving work of learning to live, work, play, and minister together. To make a difference in each other's lives and in the world. To bear God's love and to be a witness to God's presence in the world.

But remember that when weariness comes—and it will—when you want to give up, Amy, or when despair visits your life

---

[9] Peter Chelsem, director, *Shall We Dance?* (Miramax Films, 2004).

or community and you don't think you can believe anything at all. Abide. That is our calling anyway. Not to prune. Pruning is God's work. We are called to show up. To abide IN Jesus. To abide each other. (Yes, the word "abide" means this too—to put up with, wait patiently for, withstand.) To abide with each other. This is the radical friendship and community to which God calls us, the kind of community that in its way of caring for, standing by, and dwelling with becomes itself a prophetic witness to God's grace.

Abide. This is your calling, Amy, and the calling of this community of faith with whom you serve. This is our calling as the Body of Christ. Abide. Abide because Jesus has called us friends and opened our hearts to limitless love. Abide. By the grace of God, hand in hand with each other, and in the power of the Holy Spirit that grafts us onto the true vine to bear abundant, nourishing, and taste-tingling fruit of unlimited kinds.

Doxology

Bean Row Liturgies and Free Listening

The pastures of the wilderness overflow, the hills gird themselves with joy, the meadows clothe themselves with flocks, the valleys deck themselves with grain; they shout and sing together for joy.

—Psalm 65:12-13

Free Listening

You can't know what story
the shell longs to tell of the sea
without holding it to your ear.
And what of pulses that slow
as life flows out into uncaring streets
or of hearts bruised and broken
that still flutter for justice?
Some truths whisper,
quiet as breath.
To hear them,
we must lean in close
and listen.
For free.

—Jill Crainshaw

"We need more sermons about kale."

When third-year divinity student Danny made this pronouncement in his sermon for our school's chapel service, the gathered worshipers laughed. Danny laughed too. But worshipers knew that Danny was serious. Danny is a gardener-theologian. He celebrates connections between worship, faith, and the earth and invites others to celebrate with him.

Danny's call to worshipers in chapel that day illumines themes at the heart of this book. We do need more sermons about kale, because we need in our worship to imagine and experience more concrete links between the stuff of worship and the stuff of the earth. We need reminders that the cycles of life, death, and resurrection we name and celebrate during the Lord's meal are also the cycles of the earth, of human existence, of everyday living.

But worship does more than *remind* worshipers of links between spirituality and life's cycles and rhythms. Worship *orients* us toward God, the world, and others in life-savoring and life-saving ways.

Liturgical theologian James K. A. Smith says that ritual is "the way we learn to believe with our bodies."[1] The invitation of this book is for worship leaders and worshipers to design worship with a new intentionality and awareness of worship's full-bodied formational possibilities. Worship shapes who we are, what we see and think about ourselves, God, and the world, and what we do each day as people working to embody God's grace.

Worship's formational possibilities began to take hold for me the first time I served as an acolyte in my Lutheran church. I was seven or eight years old. I had been looking forward to lighting the candles in church for a long time. Until then, I had only watched from a church pew while other children marched forward in their acolyte robes to

---

[1] Smith, *Imagining the Kingdom*, 92.

ignite the two candles on the altar. I looked forward to the day when I was old enough to light those candles.

On my first day as an acolyte, I was surprised by what I became privy to that was behind the scenes of our church's worship service. The robes and candlelighters were kept in a room just off the chancel area. I had never been in this room before and was fascinated to see up close the white table linens I had only seen from a distance. The linens were all folded and stacked in a cupboard, waiting their turn to be used. That side room had a sink too, and the tiny glasses that people drank from during Communion were upside down in neat rows on a towel next to the sink. Looking very conspicuous to me in that holy place was a quite ordinary looking bottle of dish detergent.

"That's like our sink at home," I thought. "Someone has to wash all of those glasses."

Seeing these holy worship things in the side room awakened something in me. The next time I washed supper glasses in the kitchen sink at our house, I was surprised to find myself thinking about those tiny Communion cups by the sink in that room at church. A connection had been made, subtle but enduring. I saw dishwashing as if for the first time much as I had seen Holy Communion in that side room as if for the first time. At the time, I could not give words to what the connection meant, but my body recognized it.

The power of worship is its capacity to shape our embodied predispositions to all dimensions of life. Smith argues that everyday actions and worship actions are habituated actions that influence our desires and motivate what we do.[2] And the two—daily habits and worship habits—can and do influence each other. The aim is for us to pay more attention to both—the stuff of life and the stuff of worship—and be more intentional in helping worshipers to recognize and experience the connections between them. The aim is for us to see

---

[2] Ibid.

behind the scenes of worship what is common and ordinary about worship's holy things *and* for us to see behind the scenes of daily life and recognize the holiness in common and ordinary everyday things.

Two outcomes result: first, as Smith says, worship instills in our bodies—in our bones—the story of the Gospel. Our disposition to the world is shaped on a daily basis, Smith writes, by "the stories that have captivated us, have sunk into our bones. . . . We live into the stories we have absorbed; we become characters in the stories that have captivated us."[3] The stories Smith means here are cultural stories—the ongoing everyday stories of consumerism, politics, race, gender, and economics that infuse the rituals we live each day. The Gospel story, he continues, re-forms the "story in our bones." The Gospel story re-orients our lives—body, mind, and spirit—to the world in new ways.[4]

Striking about Smith's insight is his recognition of how the Gospel story is *formed* in us over time as our bodies *perform* it: "We don't memorize the Story as told to us. We imbibe the Story as we perform it in a million little gestures."[5]

What does it mean to perform the Gospel? Smith argues that knowledge about God dwells in our bodies. This means those of us in worshiping communities can begin to recognize what we do as we walk, eat, drink, wash, build, plant, touch, lift, sit, and stand each day—we can begin to see these actions as theological and spiritual because we also do them in worship in the presence of God and in the hearing of God's Story.

The reverse is also true. We read in Isaiah's call story his experience of hearing the seraphim call out to each other, "The earth is full of God's glory." Poet Elizabeth Barrett Browning's words, cited in the Prelude, come to mind again: "Earth's crammed with heaven.

[3] Ibid., 32.
[4] Ibid., 110.
[5] Ibid.

And every common bush afire with God."[6] In worship, we celebrate the sacredness of everyday things because we have learned to listen and look for God in our daily lives.

Gerald was one of the sages who taught me something about this truth, about this bond between the actions of worship and how we move through the world each day. Gerald was a member of the first church I pastored. When I arrived at the church fresh out of seminary to meet the folks at the church during worship on my interview weekend, Gerald was the first person to greet me. He was the first person to greet everyone who came to worship.

A retired insurance salesperson, Gerald had for many years longed to be a pastor, but his family obligations prevented him from following this dream. He instead embodied his passion each Sunday morning by arriving early and greeting every person who came through the church doors with a bold "hello" and a gripping handshake. By the time worship began each Sunday, Gerald had made his way along every pew in the sanctuary to shake hands and talk with church members and visitors.

When I first became pastor at the church, I had a hard time feeling connected to Gerald. He and I held rather different theological perspectives, and I did not know quite what to make of his Sunday morning welcoming ritual. I felt a distance between us, but I didn't know what to do about it.

My sense of connectedness to Gerald shifted one Tuesday morning when I stopped by to visit him and his wife of forty years, Melva. ˑa had been diagnosed with cancer some months earlier. No ˑnts had been effective, and she was dying. When I arrived ˑand Melva's home that Tuesday, Gerald was outside in his

ˑett Browning, "Aurora Leigh," in *The Oxford Book of English* ˑ H. S. Nicholson and A. H. E. Lee (Oxford: The Clarendon ˑble at www.bartleby.com/236/ (accessed October 16, 2016).

vegetable garden. He was an avid gardener with an emerald-green thumb. During the summer, Gerald often ornamented his welcoming ritual with an offer of cucumbers and tomatoes. He brought the vegetables with him to church and shared them freely with worshipers. The morning I arrived at Gerald's for a visit, Gerald was bent over in his bean patch, a floppy straw hat on his head.

Gerald greeted me with his usual Sunday "hello" and handshake. I remember thinking that Gerald's everyday greeting was the same as his Sunday greeting.

"Come on out here and pick yourself a few beans," he said.

I walked out through the row where Gerald was working. The bean plants were bowing to the ground from their abundance of ripe beans. As I picked some beans and began to put them in his gathering basket, Gerald started to talk. I heard a catch in his voice and looked up. His eyes were filled with tears. Melva's illness was breaking his heart.

He kept picking beans. I did too. I don't recall what else we said, just that we worked there together in the bean rows, our faces and backs warmed by the Tuesday morning sun. I remember noticing Gerald's arthritic hands and thinking for the first time how painful it must be to pick beans—and to shake all of those hands at church every Sunday. I imagined those same gnarled hands attending to Melva with persistent care.

Once the gathering basket was full of beans, both Gerald and I stood up to stretch. Gerald looked up toward the sky. When he spoke, I wasn't sure if it was to me or to no one in particular or perhaps just to the God of string beans: "If I wanted to paint God's love for me and Melva and our family on the heavens for all the world to see, I would need a bigger sky."

The liturgy in the bean rows I experienced that day changed m[e] and transformed my relationship with Gerald. Gerald's bean r[ow] liturgy was not all that different from his Sunday morning chu[rch] row liturgy. I saw the liturgy again when Gerald and I went in[to] his house to Melva's bedside and I saw how he took her hand in his arthritic one. Gerald's very body carried in it a Gospel story of God's "bigger than the sky" love for him and for others.

We need more sermons about kale and more bean-row liturgies in these days when so much that happens in our world seems devoid of God's big-sky love and grace. Increasing instances of violence on city streets, the needless deaths of men, women, and children of color, the harsh and deadly realities refugees face daily across the globe, the presence of growling bellies in first-grade classrooms—images of all of these painful realities and more flood the news media and our senses every day. The danger? That we will become numb to the pain, our hearts inoculated against the soul-piercing truths of these lived experiences because we imbibe them in a million little sound bites without ever really listening or encountering their depths.

I am a Presbyterian minister living in North Carolina. Many clergy, some of whom are colleagues and friends, headed out into the Charlotte streets on September 20, 2016, after Keith Lamont Scott, an African American man, was shot and killed by police. They wanted to join peaceful protests and offer words of care and support to people who were angry or frightened or upset.

On my Facebook newsfeed one day not long after Keith Scott was killed was a photo of a Charlotte clergywoman, Erika Funk, holding a sign that said "free listening" (#urbanconfessional, #listeningmat-rs). The message of that sign has stayed with me. Does anyone 'y listen anymore?

﹥ noise that bombards our ears day in and day out makes it hard
Less than a week after Keith Scott's death, the disruptive raucous presidential debate and the endless spinning that 'urated living rooms and social media. The following idential debate was even noisier with its strident ﹥tion and talking over each other and the debate

moderator. Again, I found myself asking: Does anyone listen anymore? Do I listen?

The Gospel calls us to the work of listening, open-hearted, awe-sparked listening to each other and especially to voices on the margins, to those silenced by systemic injustice. And the gift of listening is relationships that heal and transform lives and communities. That was the Gospel call and promise Erika Funk's presence and sign proclaimed without speaking a word.

Talk is too easy and can become little more than meaningless noise. But listening? When we tune our ears to the world around us, we take a stance of attentive care for others. We resist endless empty chatter. Worship can form in us such a stance. Worship can teach us to pay attention to how God is present in all of life and in each person's life.

And what we encounter in the world each day—when we embrace the truth that God's creative spirit infuses all creation and that God became flesh and dwelt among us—can form in us the capacity to see God anew in the water, wine and bread of worship, and in the people with whom we gather to sing praises. Along with the psalmist, we can be "awed by God's signs" in the people and the world around us. Then, transformed, we can go forth each day with wonder and delight as our traveling companions, renewed in our calling to join God in God's work to redeem the world.